James C. Newsham.

A CONCISE GUIDE TO POLO

A CONCISE GUIDE TO
POLO

JNP WATSON

Foreword by
Brigadier P T Thwaites

· THE ·
SPORTSMAN'S
PRESS
LONDON

Published by The Sportman's Press, 1989

British Library Cataloguing in Publication Data
Watson, J. N. P. (John N. P.)
A concise guide to polo
1. Polo
I. Title
796.35'3

ISBN 0–948253–33–9

Photoset and printed in Great Britain
by Redwood Burn Limited, Trowbridge, Wiltshire

CONTENTS

ACKNOWLEDGEMENTS

The author would like to thank the following for permission to reproduce photographs:

Michael Chevis (Plates 2, 4, 8 (below), 9 (above), 11 (below), 13).

Stanley Hurwitz (Plate 16 (below)).

Mike Roberts (Plates 1, 3, 5, 6, 7, 8 (above), 9 (below), 10, 11 (above), 12, 14).

LIST OF PLATES

FOREWORD

Polo has come a long way since it was defined in my youth, as 'a game played by peers on the other side of the ground'. Today, whilst still all too often played on the far side of the ground, it is played by a much wider section of the population, from ten year olds in the Pony Club, to farmers, tycoons, young and old and full-time professionals. Every year, in spite of the increasing pressures of time and money, new clubs are formed and new players join the ranks of the Hurlingham Polo Association.

I am delighted to write the Foreword to this book. John Watson is the most distinguished writer on horses and equine sports in this country and his wide experience of polo – meticulously observed at every level – uniquely qualifies him to give expert guidance to anyone wishing to learn more about the game.

This is an ideal guide for all those who would like to take up polo, or who have already started but want to widen their knowledge of the game. It is all here, in most concise and readable form: the qualities required of both man and horse; the strokes and skills; the characteristics of both individual and team play – all the complexities of this greatest of all games. The interpretation of the rules is clear and concise and well supported by excellent diagrams and photographs. The author's advice to 'start young' is particularly apposite. Three out of the four members of the recent England International teams started their polo in the Pony Club. Any would-be player taking up the game after the age of thirty will have a lot of fun and spend a lot of money, but he is unlikely to achieve a high-goal rating.

This is a most valuable book, a worthy companion to John Watson's *World of Polo* and one which will be of help to polo players for years to come.

Brigadier P. T. Thwaites
Chairman of the Hurlingham Polo Association

AUTHOR'S NOTE

This simple explanation of polo is designed as a manual for those who are thinking of taking up the game, to give them some idea of the time, dedication, effort and money involved in that exciting adventure. I hope that both aficionados and potential poloists will find these pages a pleasure to read.

My sincere thanks are due to four very experienced players who took great trouble in reading through the typescripts and making many useful suggestions. They are Grant Boyd-Gibbins, Patrick Churchward MRCVS, Edward Horswell and Somerville Livingstone-Learmonth, instructor at the Guards Polo Club.

1

UNDERSTANDING THE GAME

Polo is a dashing sport in every sense of that adjective. At its best it is perhaps reminiscent in its speed, dash and excitement of the pictures we know of brisk cavalry skirmishes or, in its rhythm, of musical rides. It is unique in its colour and glamorous aura; it is like a hectic equestrian ballet.

A LOVELY GAME TO WATCH

Any potential player would be well advised in the first instance to attend, as a critical spectator, as many good matches as possible. Entering the stand to witness a big match – of this ultra-fast ball-game – for the first time, he should sense delight at the general picture, the vivid turf, the team colours and the spick turn-out of the players, reflected in the bright bandages and saddle cloths of the beautiful well-groomed ponies; and, as play gets underway, at the skilful ball control, long hitting and the well co-ordinated team drill of the game.

Polo consists of a player driving a little wooden ball with a long and strangely balanced mallet from the back of a rushing pony, in cooperation with three other players, towards a narrow goalmouth; the opponents of those four are constantly trying to obstruct that endeavour and keep the ball to themselves with the same purpose; the play thus twists and turns relentlessly in a dizzying flurry of mallets and a stampede of ponies' feet, soon convincing the spectator that it must be the most difficult of all games to master.

He is advised to arrive 10 or 15 minutes early for a match. This should ensure a good position for his car (particularly if, in cold or wet weather he intends to watch from it) and a good central seat in the stand. Moreover, the commentator may not only announce any changes in the programme but may also have some interesting prelimi-

DIMENSIONS OF THE GROUND

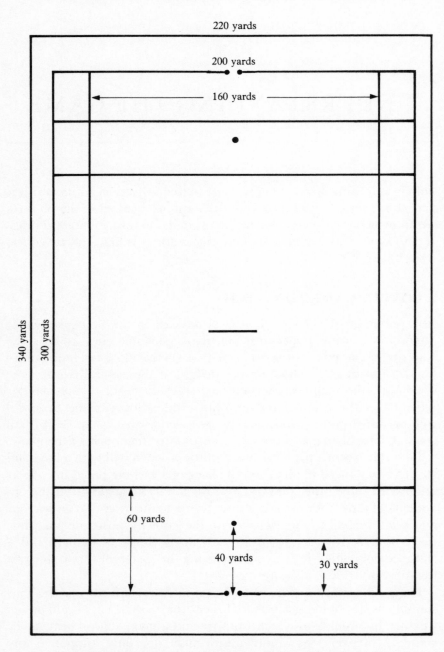

Overall length 300 yards, width 200 yards (boarded ground 160 yards). Penalty lines 30 yards and 60 yards. 'Spot', central at 40 yards. Halfway line marked with a short line.

Safety zone 10 yards beyond side boundaries: 20 yards beyond back lines.

Goal-posts are 8 yards apart.

nary comments to make on the players and the contest concerned. Early arrival may also give time to visit the pony lines, the waiting ponies and their grooms being an essential part of polo's ambience.

THE FRAMEWORK

A polo pitch (*see diagram on p.12*) is 300 yards long and 200 yards wide. To keep the ball in play as much as possible most grounds are now hemmed in by boards eleven inches high, in which case the width of the ground may be as little as 160 yards. The goal posts, which are collapsible on severe impact, are 10 feet or so high and set eight yards apart.

The ground is marked with parallel white lines, 60 yards and 30 yards from the goal lines and a central 40-yard spot. These indicate the distances of the penalty shots. The half-way point, or centre, is marked by a short line.

There should be a safety zone of at least 10 yards between the boundary and the nearest spectators and a run-out of 30 to 40 yards at each end of the ground.

The full match is divided into six 7-minute chukkas, or periods, with three minutes given in which to change ponies between chukkas. At the end of the chukka a bell is rung, but the game continues until the ball goes out of play or the $7\frac{1}{2}$ minute (second) bell is rung to end the chukka.

At half-time, that is to say after the third chukka, spectators may be invited to leave their places in the stand (assuming that the play is on grass) and help to tread in the divots while the players take a longer rest (five minutes or more). If the spectator has a dog with him this is a moment to give it a run. (During play it will either have been left in the car – with plenty of open window – or it will be on a lead sitting quietly and obediently by his side. Loose dogs on a polo ground are a danger-ous menace.)

The timings given above suggest that a six-chukka match lasts little over an hour, but the umpire's whistle inevitably dictates otherwise. A six-chukka game generally continues for over an hour-and-a-half. The clock at the end of the ground, if there is one, shows how each 7-minute chukka is passing. Next to the clock spectators should also be told, in large figures, which chukka is being played and the score.

Medium-goal, intermediate- and low-goal matches are normally of five or four chukkas, with treading-in, respectively, after the third or second chukka.

THE PLAYER

Polo expertise derives more from the combination of a naturally athletic style, the gift of good co-ordination of eye and limb and a flair for ball games than it does from good horsemanship. The successful player would be good, if he tried, at cricket, hockey, tennis or squash.

But he will also contrive, of course, to become a very good horseman, at once strong and sensitive. He will endeavour to forge himself and his pony into a single component, with all the empathy which that implies.

AIM

The ball, coloured white, weighs $4\frac{1}{2}$ oz and is $3\frac{1}{2}$ in in diameter. Balls are more usually composed of plastic than the traditional bamboo nowadays. The objective is to hit the ball between the opposition's posts and to prevent them passing it between one's own posts. The side scoring most goals wins.

PONIES

Each player draws on a number of ponies, not less than two. A pony should not be called upon to play more than two chukkas per game, and never two chukkas running. Few spectators appreciate that good ponies are just as important to the game as good players. The term 'pony' as against 'horse' is traditional, dating from the days when there was a height limit. Ponies are discussed more fully in Chapter Two.

EQUIPMENT

The polo mallet, or stick, is comprised of a bamboo shaft and a hard wooden head. The ball is struck with the face of the head, not the end. The length of the stick will depend upon the height of the pony, and the player's height and length of arm; 48–53 inches are the standard, 51–52 inches the average. For reasons of safety no poloist may play with his left hand.

Safety caps or helmets must be worn at all times, and most players don leather knee-pads. Traditionally, breeches are white and boots brown. Depending upon the character of the pony, blunt spurs (without rowels) are, or are not, worn, and whips carried.

TEAM POSITIONS

The four team positions will be dealt with in depth in Chapter Three. In brief, Numbers *One* and *Two* are the forwards; the number *Three* position (the equivalent of half-back in soccer) is generally held by the team captain and/or strongest team member. He is the pivot man upon whom the whole team hinges. In principle, the *Back* is responsible for defence. As a general rule the Number *One* and the opposing *Back* are responsible for marking one another, while the *Twos* are responsible for marking the *Threes* and vice versa. However, as the essence of good team play is flexibility and interplay, the positions are essentially interchangeable, the criterion for that being players' team knowledge and instinct.

These principles regarding team positions are enlarged upon in Chapter Three.

HANDICAPS

In the programme, the team position with the player's name alongside it is followed by a second number, perhaps in brackets. That is the handicap. A tyro starts his career, on his club handicap list, at –2, the world's highest rating being +10. Different players are referred to in a variety of jargon: a '10-goaler', 'an 8-goal player', a 'minus one', 'playing off a six-goal handicap', 'rated at four, etc, goals'.

The word 'goal' in each case, does not, of course, indicate how many times the player is expected to score, but only implies his value to the team. Players find their places in teams – high-goal, medium-goal, intermediate- or low-goal – according to their standards.

TEAM HANDICAP

It is by collective handicaps that team strengths are judged. In the programme the individual handicaps are totalled to give the team aggregate rating. If the addition comes to, say, 19, we call it a 19-goal team.

In the Argentine national championships there may be two 40-goal squads in opposition. At the other end of this scale in European low-goal class polo a spectator might witness a 2-goal team against a 3-goal (eg. two minus ones, a plus 4 and a 0 versus a −2, a 3 and a two +1s). But he should only watch it if he must from loyalty to one or more of the players, because he would not find it very inspiring, and might be put off polo permanently! British high-goal tournaments are normally open to 17–22 goal teams, medium-goal, 12–15; intermediate 8–12; and low, 4–8, or lower.

HANDICAP TOURNAMENTS

Tournaments and matches may be played either on an open or a handicap basis. If on handicap, the number of goals' start – accorded to a team of lesser handicap in any particular match – is arrived at by multiplying the difference between the two teams' total handicaps by the number of chukkas being played, and dividing that figure by six. Any fraction counts as half a goal. Suppose, for example, in a six-chukka handicap tournament, if a 22-goal team faces a 20-goal team the latter receives 2 goals. Or, in the case of a 17-goal team against a 21-goal team, over five chukkas, the 17-goal team starts with $3\frac{1}{2}$ on the scoreboard (i.e. $21-17=4$, $4\times5=20$, $20\div6=3\frac{1}{2}$).

TEAM BALANCE

A well-balanced team – put in the simplest terms – is one in which the four places are filled by players of a fairly level standard. In a badly balanced team the work is inclined to be poorly distributed, with the high handicaps doing much of the work of the more inferior players as well as their own. A 20-goal squad, for example, is better served by, say two 6s, a 5 and a 3, than by a 9, an 8, a 2 and a 1. From the spectator's viewpoint matches between well-balanced teams are that much more interesting and instructive.

PONY POWER

One team may be superior in collective handicaps, another in ponies. Clearly a very well mounted team has a marked advantage over one

Plate 1 (*above*) The throw-in. Amongst the players are (*from left to right*) Gabriel Donoso of Chile (handicap 8), Cody Forsyth of New Zealand (7) and the Marquess of Milford Haven (3). (*below*) Tussle for the ball from a throw-in. On the left is the American 8-goaler, Rob Walton.

Plate 2 A shot from the pony's nearside.

Plate 3 More shots from the nearside: Julian Hipwood (handicap 8) is the player in the lower picture.

Plate 4 Paul Withers, the Cowdray Park veteran (handicap 7) with a shot from the pony's offside.

Plate 5 Another offside shot: HRH The Prince of Wales (handicap 4) and (*behind*), the Marquess of Milford Haven (3).

Plate 6 Riding off. Britain's top handicap, Howard Hipwood (9), is in possession of the ball.

Plate 7   (*above*) Anticipation. Simon Tomlinson (handicap 4), of the Los Locos team is in possession here (*third from the right*).

(below) On the boards. The man with the ball is Lt-Col Reddy Watt (*middle*), who plays off a 5 handicap.

Plate 8   Attempting to hook.

that is playing on relatively indifferent ponies. On the other hand moderate horsemen will often extract less from expensive, and potentially very handy, mounts than high-handicap men get out of their run-of-the-mill ponies.

The spectator may hear the commentator remark that so-and-so is 'on a very fast pony'. Frequently that is not the case at all, but rather that the player in question, a masterly polo horseman, knows just how to squeeze the ultimate turn of speed out of a quite ordinary mount and – which is often more important – how to turn him more tightly and more sharply, while the opponent he is chasing and challenging for the ball is on a flyer, but has neither the confidence to let it go full tilt, nor the expertise to turn it in loose-rein pirouettes like his rival.

Be that as it may, pony power counts for a great deal in team strength and it adds much interest for the spectator if he will learn, in watching matches, to evaluate the usefulness of the ponies on either side.

UMPIRES

The game is conducted by two mounted umpires, invariably very experienced players. They are distinguished from the teams' colours by wearing shirts of black and white vertical stripes. On the sideline – or preferably high on the spectators' stand where he has a bird's-eye view of the game – there will also be a referee, to whom the umpires appeal if they disagree.

The umpires should be sufficiently well mounted to enable them to keep close to the game without having to think about riding their ponies. They will, of course, always keep out of the way of the players.

Before the game begins each will agree to be responsible for one goal line and one side line and to take charge roughly of one half of the ground. Polo being ruled by 'the Right of Way' (a principle to which we will come in a moment), the ideal is for one umpire to be continually behind the ball and the other perpendicular with it.

The umpires are served at each end by goal judges who look after the goal posts and wave a flag to signal the scoring of a goal. There should be two at each goal for the more important matches. But in cases where the ball passes very close to one of the posts an umpire may be in a better position to judge and may therefore over-rule the goal judges' verdict.

HOW CROSSES ARE COMMITTED

1. The white player is about to cross his opponent's line and will therefore be committing a serious and dangerous infringement.

3. The white player may move parallel with the line and play a shot, providing he can do so without interfering with black's mount or causing him to check back.

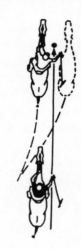

2. When travelling in the same direction the white player may draw level with black and then force him across the line and take possession of the ball without committing a foul.

4. Two players riding for a ball from opposite directions in the open must both give way to the left and take the ball on their right or offside.

5. When two players are approaching the ball in the open from different directions, the player approaching at the least angle to the line of the ball has the right of way.

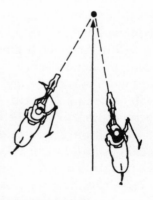

AND HOW AVOIDED

RULES TO PROTECT THE PONIES

The rules of the game are laid down specifically for the safety of the ponies – to avoid collision or dangerous use of sticks, and to defend against unwitting injury.

As a start it is re-emphasised that no player may wield his stick in the left hand.

Ponies have their tails tied up, to prevent a stick, or another pony's tack, becoming entangled.

Ponies' legs have to be either bandaged or provided with protective boots.

Above all 'the Right of Way' must be respected.

THE RIGHT OF WAY

The governing law of the game is that a player having hit the ball is entitled to follow the line of that ball to take a further shot. This Right of Way exists at each and every moment of the game (except, of course, when the ball is out of play) and is always considered to extend ahead of the player who owns it. But the Right of Way is not to be confused with the Line of the Ball, nor does it explicitly depend upon who was the last striker.

Possession of the Right of Way entitles the player to take the ball on the offside (right side) of his pony. If he changes his direction to take it on the nearside, and thereby endangers another player who would have been clear to take it on his offside, he loses his Right of Way and must keep clear of the other.

It follows that no player may cross the Right of Way or enter it except at such a distance that there is no danger of a collision, nor any interference with the stroke of the player who is in possession of it.

Players who are riding from opposite directions on the exact line of the ball must keep to the left, i.e. each must take, or attempt to take, the ball on their offside.

If nobody is on the exact line of the ball the player following its direction at the narrowest angle is entitled to the Right of Way, though his line may cross the line of the ball. If no player is riding in the general direction of the ball near enough to risk a collision with players riding to meet it, the Right of Way passes to the player meeting the ball at the narrowest angle.

MORE TABOOS

I. It is forbidden to hit across the legs of a pony.

II. The elbow may not be used when riding off.

III. A player may hook an opponent's stick but never across a pony or above the shoulders.

If a player can enter the line of the ball in front of another riding on the line – far enough in front to avoid any risk of collision – he may do so, but he must not then check his pony. Having occupied that position he owns the Right of Way.

No player may check or pull up on the Right of Way; nor may he cross it if by doing so he risks collision with the player entitled to it.

RIDING OFF

A player may challenge for possession by pushing his opponent off the line of the ball by laying his pony alongside and using its weight to push him away. But endeavouring this by meeting a pony at a wide angle, or by charging dangerously, is not permitted. Nor may a player use his elbow to ride off.

Riding off is an important part of marking – in all players' attempts to keep the upper hand by edging their opposite numbers away from the ball (or from his team mates). A spectator will soon see that riding off constitutes a principal element of the game.

HOOKING

A player may also interfere with an opponent in possession of the ball by hooking his stick while playing a shot, but this is only permitted below shoulder height and not across either the body or legs of the opponent's pony.

It is good polo to hook an opponent's stick or to deflect his stroke by interposing the stick, but it may only be done from the side on which the opponent is attempting his stroke. Nor may a wide swipe be taken at the opponent's stick.

INFRINGEMENTS, OR FOULS

So 'crossing' and 'foul hooking' are polo's two principal infringements. Others are zigzagging in front of a player so as to cause him to check; pulling across the forelegs of an opponent's pony so as to risk tripping it; riding at a player in such a manner as to cause him to pull up or miss his stroke (in other words, intimidation); hitting across the forelegs of an opponent's pony; hitting into, or among, the legs of ponies, and other dangerous uses of the stick.

The foul of 'dangerous riding' is most often made when a player hits a nearside backhander, because many players when making this shot throw their weight over and this forces their ponies across the line of the ball. 'Dangerous riding', too, is riding out of control, or intentionally ramming an opponent.

APPEALING FOR FOULS

'Appealing' is not allowed. All too often spectators will see a player raise his stick, claiming he has been fouled. Or, worse still, shouting with the same intent. Appealing is unsportsmanlike and a breach of good manners, and a habit that grew increasingly rife during the 1980s. Umpires should ignore it unless it becomes intolerable from a particular player, in which case they should remonstrate sternly, and not put up with it again.

PLAYING FOR FOULS

The worst of all unsportsmanlike behaviour is the pernicious trick of playing for a foul, that is to say deliberately causing an opponent to commit an infringement in order to gain a penalty shot. Such a practice is severely frowned upon.

The Hurlingham Polo Association recently incorporated the following stricture in the Field Rules as further guidance to umpires on one aspect of the 'manufactured foul': 'if a player with possession of the ball, or right to the line of the ball on his offside, checks his speed to such an extent that an opposing player may enter the line and take the ball on his offside, without, in the opinion of the umpires, creating any danger to the checking player, if that player were to *maintain* his reduced speed, then no foul shall be deemed to have occurred, even if the checking player subsequently increases his speed. Umpires are advised that if the checking player slows to a walk, or stops completely, under this directive, it is almost impossible for any danger to occur, and therefore, no foul is committed.'

PENALTIES

Umpires may award penalties in the following order of severity:

First, a Penalty goal. If a player commits a dangerous or deliberate foul in his team's goalmouth vicinity in order to save a goal, the side that has been fouled is given a goal. (The ball is then thrown in 10 yards in front of the goal without ends being changed.)

Second, a 30-yard hit. A free hit 30 yards from the goal line opposite the middle of the goal, or, if preferred, from where the foul occurred. The defenders to remain behind the back line (not between the goal posts) until the shot has been taken.

Penalty 3 – A free hit 40 yards from the goal line, opposite the centre of the goal, the defenders not to cross the goal line before the hit has been taken, nor to be between the goal posts.

Penalty 4 – A free hit 60 yards from the goal line of the side fouling, taken opposite the middle of the goal; the side fouling can be on the ground, but not within 30 yards of the ball until it is hit. The side fouled can place themselves where they like.

Penalty 5a – A free hit from where the ball was when the foul took place, but not nearer the boards or side lines than four yards. None of the side fouling to be within 30 yards of the ball, the side fouled being free to occupy any positions they choose.

Penalty 5b – As for 5a, but from the centre of the ground.

STARTING A GAME

The game begins with an underhand throw-in between the two teams, the *Ones* in front followed by the *Twos* and *Threes* opposite one another, with the *Backs* behind and a little out to one side.

Spectators will see the players jockeying to be first at the ball, first out of the mêlée and into the opposition's end of the ground.

WHEN THE GAME STOPS

Umpires stop the game as follows:

(a) If they consider a foul has been committed. In which case a penalty is awarded as considered appropriate, provided the other umpire agrees.

(b) If a pony falls. The game is resumed when the player re-mounts. Or, in the case of injury to the pony, when the player has secured another.

(c) At the end of the chukka.

(d) When a goal is scored. The two sides change ends and there is a throw-in from the centre of the ground.

(e) When the ball goes over the boards, or side line. The clock does not stop. The teams line up five yards from the side and there is a further throw-in.

(f) If the attackers hit the ball over the back line. The defenders take a free hit in from the point at which the ball crossed the line.

(g) If a defender hits the ball over his own back line. The attackers are awarded a free shot from the 60-yard line.

(h) If a player is injured. Play is resumed when he is ready to continue the game.

(i) If a player is injured to the extent that he cannot continue playing. Play resumes when a substitute is found.

In the case of broken tack, loose bandages, etc., the game is not stopped unless the discrepancy poses a threat to other players and ponies.

Chukkas are ended by the sounding of two bells, as already mentioned, the first after seven minutes, the second, to stop play, 30 seconds later. If the ball goes out of play after the first bell that also ends the chukka.

The game is finished by the sound of a single bell.

THE REFEREE

The referee should, like the umpires, be a very experienced player with an impeccable knowledge of the rules. He is there to arbitrate if the umpires disagree. In which case one of them will turn towards the referee and raise his hand. If, in the referee's opinion, no foul has occurred he makes a wash-out signal by a horizontal movement with both arms across his front. If he thinks a foul has been committed he raises one hand above his head, and, with the other, points in the direction in which the free hit is to be taken. If in doubt he stands up, which is the signal for the umpires to canter over to him for a consultation. If the umpires wish in any case to consult him, they will canter over to him without any preliminary signal.

A FORE AND AFT GAME

The critical observer of a polo match will be looking to see that the players are disposed, for the most part, in column, rather than on the wings (as in hockey or soccer). In good polo two players of the same side should be rarely seen level with one another, but only alongside their opposite numbers.

ALWAYS WATCH GOOD POLO

'Never watch low-goal or club polo, except the best exhibition matches unless, *noblesse oblige*, you are loyally supporting a husband, son, brother, or whatever,' is a good maxim because, if watched too often, the spectator may be put off the game altogether. For since polo has no rival as the most difficult of all games to master, the performances of the tyros will contrast embarrassingly with the supremacy of the high-flyers.

In a beginner's game, or even a low-goal match, spectators are likely to witness much poor horsemanship and stick work. Moreover, the tyros, with their endeavour to be first at the ball and their inability to send long passes, will probably spend much of the time bunched in tight throngs. Whereas good polo is open, fore-and-aft polo, in which vigilant marking, ever-ready anticipation, quick turning, masterly ball control and thoughtful interchange of positions are the hallmarks. Those characteristics, coupled with the speed of top-class ponies and brilliant riding are what makes polo worth watching – 'worth watching' for the aficionado, a 'must' for the beginner.

COMMENTARIES

In the old days commentaries, while instructive, were loud enough for the uninitiated to absorb, without being intrusive to the regular and reasonably well-informed spectator. In those days commentators did not talk unless there was something relevantly interesting to be said. Their successors, however, are expected at most clubs to be entertaining, too, and some endeavour to make their orations more rivetting than the game itself. As though half the audience is blind they inform them when the ball has been hit out of play; and as though the other half is deaf they tell them when the bell has rung to end a chukka. Some interlard their monologues with heavy jokes (but some with considerable wit!); others keep coming up with the names of ponies (which hardly stands as interesting information on its own). Admittedly, however, a higher proportion of people in the spectator stands nowadays welcome blow-by-blow accounts, well interspersed with explanatory asides on the mysteries of the game, and given with a light touch. So perhaps those who prefer to interpret the course of a match for themselves are best advised to practise the selective habit of only tuning in for particular communiqués ... or to watch from their cars with the windows tightly closed!

2

PONIES

PONY TYPE

Polo ponies are still 'ponies', notwithstanding the lifting of the 14.2 hh height limit by the Americans as long ago as 1916. We speak of a team's, or an individual's, 'pony-power' (not 'horse-power'), of the 'pony-lines' (not the 'horse-lines'). It is pony character we are looking for in the polo mount, an animal not having the long-striding, undulating action of an eventer or steeplechaser, but a low, smooth pony action, so that the base from which the stick-strokes are to be played remain relatively level. The nearer the player is to the ball, by and large, the easier it is to hit. 15.0–15.3 hh is about right. An animal of that stature will also be quicker and tighter on the turn than a 16–17 hh horse.

THE UNDER 14.2 DAYS

To understand the nature of the polo pony it is an advantage to know something of its background and sources. Before the abolition of the height limit, Britain, as the pioneer of polo in the Western world and possessing a wealth of mountain and moorland breeds, was the most sought-after source of ponies in the world and Welsh blood was to be found in most places where polo was played.

By the turn of the nineteenth century polo was a very well established game in the Argentine, and English and Irish settlers were putting mares of their ranch breed, the *criollo*, to Welsh ponies to produce strong and outstandingly handy 14.0–14.1 playing ponies. Sheep farmers in Australia made the same experiment successfully with their 'Walers' (originating in New South Wales) and many of the progeny, proving fast and handy, were bought by clubs and players of the British *raj* in India.

CRIOLLOS MOST IN DEMAND

At the time, the removal of the height limit put the British pony-breeder more or less out of business. For the Argentine rancher breeding horses has always been his stock-in-trade – breeding them for the handiness, speed and easy temperament (the first qualities of the polo pony) required for their home employment. And, having vast areas of farm-land ideal for rearing stock, they were, and are, in a position to breed them in great numbers.

With the removal of the 14.2 hh height limit the Argentines exper-imented successfully with the introduction of English Thoroughbred blood – and thus with the consequent addition of greater quality and pace – to produce the ideal 15.0–15.3 hh pony. Meanwhile players in the Army in India – of which there were nearly as many as in all the British clubs put together – welcomed the lifting of the height limit, as it enabled them to make use of the more suitable of their regimental chargers and troop horses.

In the United States, Britain and other polo-playing countries the relative expense of forage, farriery, transport, grooms' wages and veter-inary services, coupled with time consumption, rendered the rearing and making of ponies hardly worth the effort, particularly considering that good ponies could be acquired so cheaply from Argentina.

The Argentines, being able to mass-produce ponies of the right heredity and stamp, having cheap labour to look after them and cheap facilities of every kind; having, too, both the expertise and the time to break and school them – and the option to discard for the *estancia* all but the ones that turned out best – quickly cornered the polo pony market. They bred, as they still do, from dams that had proved their worth on the polo ground.

WIDENING MARKET, RISING PRICE

This situation continued until the Argentine economy got into a mess in the early 1950s. The Peron government's tariffs put up the prices of transport, by both sea and air, to such an extent that it became about as cheap to breed and make a pony in Britain as to import one from South

POINTS OF THE PONY

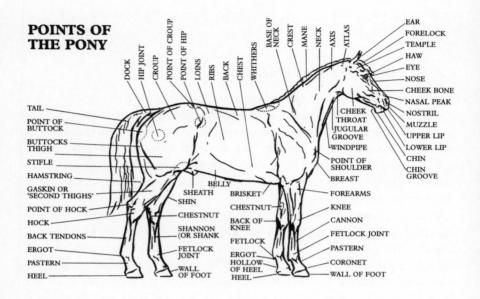

SKELETON OF THE PONY

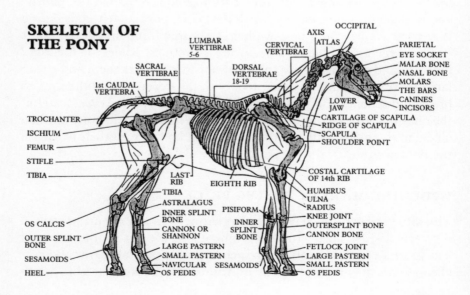

America. The situation stabilised somewhat during the 1960s, but the price of Argentinian ponies shot up once more with the oil crisis of the '70s. Freight charges escalated again and, a little later, were inflated further with the astonishing growth of the game in the United States.

In 1978 there were fewer than 2,500 American players. Within a decade of that, the number has grown to nearly 10,000. With rich Americans buying heavily in the Argentine pony market, the prices soared as never before. This new inflationary effect reverberated throughout the polo world. At the time of writing (1989) the average cost of a good medium-goal animal in Britain is in the region of £6,000–£7,000 and for a well-proved high-goal mount, £8,000–£12,000. There are some ponies bred and made in Britain, New Zealand, Australia and the United States which are fetching those prices, many of them just as good as the best Argentine products. But the Argentine market being still the readiest, most players turn in that direction for their supply. The man who has just graduated from tuition and is starting in the game, might secure his ponies for £5,000–£6,000 apiece.

THE BEGINNER'S MOUNT

The novice, however, will not be concerned with that problem for the moment. What he needs to start on is a quiet veteran stick-and-ball pony, 'a Dobbin', one for which the days of two hectic chukkas in a day, three times a week, are over. But one whose mouth has not hardened; which will still respond easily to the aids, and turn sharply on the hocks; one which has not gone ball-shy and will cooperate boldly in a practice ride-off; and play slow tuitional chukkas once or twice a week.

The tyro's club may hire him such a mount, but – most hirelings being doubtful tutors – he is better advised to have his own. He will need to ask at the club office and around the players to discover who might have such a pony for sale. Usually a beginner with only one or two ponies will keep them at a good livery stable. But he may wish to stable them at home. In which case he should make enquiries, according to his local circumstances, regarding a groom (if he cannot find one privately he will doubtless advertise), fodder, the availability of veterinary and farrier services and the expense of saddlery and everything else apertaining to the keeping and riding of horses. As a very rough guide the cost of keeping one pony is around £1,500–£2,000 a year

in Britain, not counting transport and the replacement of tack. On top
of all that will be his club subscription.

CONFORMATION

Unless he is already an old hand with horses, it is doubtful that the
aspiring polo novice will possess an eye for conformation – the animal's
shape and make, an attribute involving long experience. It is a facility
that he ought to try to acquire by looking over ponies at every opportunity, appraising their qualities and taking critical note of their faults.
There are several examples on record of excellent performers in high-
goal polo that have been weak in many respects, on certain points of
conformation and overall quality. But they are the exceptions that
prove the rule. In general, good all-round conformation indicates
soundness as well as strength, stamina and athleticism.

'Quality' is shown in the animal's limbs, head, skin and general
appearance. In particular, we say that a pony is of good conformation if
it has:

– a well-balanced, well-coupled look with a fairly short back
– depth through the heart, chest and lungs, indicating stamina and
  staying power
– muscular, well-sprung ribs
– a strong well-rounded loin ('well ribbed up')
– a deep stifle (plenty of space between the stifle and the point of the
  hip) coupled with a well let-down hock, indicating impulsion and
  athleticism behind
– a sloping shoulder and relatively upright humerus, the sign of a
  smooth even pace and action
– well rounded quarters, swelling with muscle
– clean, bony hocks
– clean, well-sinewed cannon-bones
– springy pasterns – neither too vertical, nor too sloping
– a well-shaped round foot, indicating hoof soundness
– a strong, muscly neck, with the hint of a curve on it
– a 'kind eye', indicating a good temperament

The prospective buyer will want the pony walked and trotted before
having it saddled for trial stick-and-ball. He will watch for an easy
swinging walk and see that it goes smoothly and straight at the trot.

BUYING RIGHT

Whatever animal he buys, whether for beginner's stick-and-ball or, later on, for the season's tournaments, he will need to try out his potential purchase before parting with his money. He will satisfy himself that it is sound; that it has a good responsive temperament; that it does not play up; that it has a soft mouth; that it goes smoothly and confidently on the bit with its hocks well under it and that it is not too much of a handful. (It is fatal for the tyro to overmount himself. High-goal horsemen have no difficulty in managing brilliant ponies that beginners may be totally lost on.)

He will judge, too, whether it is up to his weight and suitable to his height, and whether there is a comfortable empathy and feeling of goodwill between himself and the prospective purchase. He should find out whether it will stable and box easily, and behave well when tied up, and in the company of other ponies. And, of course, he will want to know its precise age and, as far as possible, its history. It should scarcely be necessary to add that to play safe it is preferable to have the advice of a friend who is a good polo horseman before concluding the deal. Either way it should never be agreed without a proper veterinary examination and a bill of clean health. (It might have a defect – as, for example, a cataract – which, though giving no trouble as such during the purchaser's tenure of it, may prove an embarrassment when he comes to sell it on, because the vet won't then pass it. And what is the insurance value of a £60 vet fee compared with the price of a pony?)

SCHOOLING

The schooling of ponies is out of the scope of this guide. For the beginner will be starting on a well-made animal and probably continuing his career on well-made mounts. But, since he will be asking his pony to carry out certain movements in certain ways it is as well that he has a fundamental knowledge of how the animal was originally ridden and then taught those movements. That is to say it is important that he should be aware of what has gone into the making of a polo pony.

We are talking of a highly-tuned, sensitive athlete, which was probably lunged, then broken to the saddle at the age of a little more than two. It was then advanced to simple training, stopping, starting, neck-reining, turning, going from the collected walk to the extended walk, from that to the trot, and from the trot to the canter. It will have had a polo stick swung around its head and body, to get it accustomed to that before proceeding to the ball. Then, to heighten its response, to strengthen it – and, also, ultimately to prepare it for riding off – it should have been taught such simple dressage exercises as the shoulder-in and the half-pass. It will be taught, with the correct use of the aids, to stop dead in its tracks at the gallop. At the age of four, perhaps, it will have been further schooled in practice chukkas before going into match play the following year.

In all that career it has been responding to correct horsemanship, never, we hope, without the aids correctly applied. A great deal of good can be undone from mishandling by an ignorant or inept rider. That is why it is imperative that any newcomer to its back applies the aids in the right way at the right moment. To get the best out of his pony, the player must become quickly acquainted with the animal's character and know its particular idiosyncrasies.

CARE

A polo player who leaves everything to the groom is a neglectful horsemaster. It is up to him to see that the tack is fitting properly and comfortably; to inspect his ponies for injury, or signs of discomfort after play; to see them rugged up – and if travelling – boxed up.

Injuries come largely from knocks, and most of those are probably on the legs. A player should get into the habit of running a hand down the legs to feel for heat or swelling, if that is suspected. He should examine the feet, too. And he should know that ponies are susceptible to back injury from riding off, especially from opponents who ride off (wrongly) behind the saddle.

The player should also take the ultimate responsibility for such matters as the stabling, bedding, feeding, watering and shoeing of his ponies, however well and truly those responsibilities are delegated. And he should know about such annual requirements as worming, clipping and tetanus and 'flu injections. Some of the books listed in the bibliography (p. 77) give detailed advice on horsemastership.

EXERCISE

Like the human athlete the polo pony needs to be kept fit and hard for its job. Thoughtful feeding and long slow work are the first keys to success. The beginner's 'Dobbin' needs nothing more than its hour's hack every day. But a pony that is to spend the summer regularly in fast tournament play requires a great deal more.

From the time it comes up from grass in the spring the pony's daily exercise should be gradually increased to one-and-a-half or two hours walking and trotting, and that should be its daily stint for a month (including as much uphill work as possible) before starting its season in chukkas. By the start of the season the pony should probably be having an hour's walking and trotting and 15–20 minutes cantering a day. Obviously the more the player exercises the pony himself the better it will be for mount and man (assuming he is a competent rider).

SUCCESS THROUGH AFFECTION

Finally, the most willing and generally satisfactory ponies are produced by discipline in tandem with kindness; a blend of firmness, affection and loving care. Only the player who feels and shows a genuine love for his ponies will be truly at one with them in the game.

3

STARTING TO PLAY

Not much in the way of the written word concerning any game can replace personal oral guidance and demonstration from a professional instructor, or other well-qualified veteran player, coupled with practice and the hard tutelage of the game itself. The following notes, therefore, are designed only to give the potential player an idea of what to expect at the start of his polo career and the principles which should be imprinted on his mind throughout it.

As to the purchase, or hire, of ponies, he will do best – according to his whereabouts, his budget, his height and weight and other circumstances – to seek the advice of his instructor.

SADDLERY AND EQUIPMENT

In simplest terms ponies carry comfortably fitting saddles, designed for the polo seat, double bridles and standing martingales. Boots or bandages are compulsory, and should also be worn for stick-and-ball practice. Ponies may not be played without tail bandages. Players, by convention, wear helmets, brown boots, white breeches, brown leather knee-pads, gloves and close-fitting shirts or vests. (Black boots are frowned upon because the stain they leave on opponents' breeches is more difficult to remove.) Coloured 'breeches' are acceptable for practice games. Face guards are a matter of personal choice. It is hoped that the beginner will not require spurs, but it is as well for him to carry a polo whip from the start as it will accustom him, as second nature, to holding that as well as the reins. The subject of sticks is dealt with on p 38. A list of (1989) prices of polo clothing and equipment is given on page 75.

LEARN TO RIDE, THEN PLAY

This chapter assumes that the reader can ride and is thoroughly acquainted with the equestrian aids. Also that he has fundamental knowledge of horsemastership, and knows what tack each pony will require. By the time the tyro rides onto the ground for his first practice game he must be a safe and competent horseman. He should be thinking exclusively by then of the duties of his team position. So rule number one is that he must not start playing until he can forget about his pony and concentrate entirely on the ball and the game.

SYMPATHETIC HORSEMANSHIP, SOUND HORSEMASTERSHIP

To begin that happy situation he needs his pony's total cooperation, and he will not have that unless he is a 'kind' horseman. A pony will not be much in sympathy with the player, for example, if the latter rides in such a way as to give it a sore back; or nervously tugs at its head, at the same time urging it to a greater speed; or jerks it in the mouth as he swivels his shoulders to strike the ball.

The hard mouths of so many hirelings which even the most experienced horsemen find difficult to stop or turn, are a testimony to how badly they have been treated by inept riders. From other mounts, nappy or cowardly, the habit of shying from the ball as the stick is raised suggests, to say the least, that they have been struck on the legs once too often! Ball-shy ponies are useless unless by coaxing them back to the ball in a gradual re-education, they can be got out of the habit. In general, polo ponies are like humans; the better they are treated, the more willing and amenable they will be.

So the player ought always to respect their welfare both in stables and in the club lines, on exercise or at grass. And, if he also respects it when he is practising his strokes and in the turmoil of his beginners' games, that will soon become like second nature to him on the ground, and he may focus all his attention on his polo.

THE ONE TO START ON

If the aspirant is to make reasonable progress towards an honourable

place on the handicap list he will begin his career on a pony that is at
once quiet and well schooled, and one that is willing to lend all its
weight and velocity in the 'ride off'.

GOOD SEAT

The player ought to take the greatest trouble from the start to acquire a
good seat. A useful polo seat is not quite the same as the expression
might imply for other equestrian purposes. Polo requires excellent
balance. Since the player rises in the stirrups to strike the ball, his
leathers will be shorter than, say, most foxhunters' or pony trekkers'.
On the other hand he will not enjoy the balance he needs if he rides as
short, for example, as a showjumper; for polo is a game of much
stopping and starting, quick turning and riding off. To strike the ball
with a good swing and follow-through, the player must turn fluently
from the waist and shoulders. A good seat also enables him to lean well
out of the saddle at a fast gallop. To improve his balance and the
security of his seat, to strengthen his riding muscles – muscles that are
rarely otherwise used – he should ride (trot) regularly without stirrups.

Flexibility – or elasticity – coupled with physical fitness, is the first
key to successful polo riding. The budding player should endeavour to
acquire the supple waist that enables him to move the upper and lower
parts of his body independently. The second key to successful polo
riding may be summed up in the words 'hands'.

GOOD HANDS

The beginner to whom this book is addressed, being already an ad-
equate horseman, will know that the 'aids' are the signals – leg, hand,
voice and the disposal of body weight – by which he conveys his wishes
to his mount. Following on from what has already been stated concerning the player's regard for his pony's mouth, it may be safely said that
'good hands' are particularly important in polo.

Bad hands, besides spoiling a pony's mouth for polo, are an in-
humane infliction on the poor creature. A good mouth is a sensitive
mouth, picking up the lightest signal transmitted through the rider's
will to his left hand, and from his hand through the reins to the bit. In
turning to keep an eye on the progress of the game, as well as to strike
the ball, the slack of the reins is being constantly taken up and released.

When that happens the player should, to avoid jerking on the pony's mouth, ride with as long a rein as is consistent with sound control.

By 'good hands' the intuitive horseman establishes that vital sympathy between himself and his pony which makes for a centaur-like composition of mount and rider. The fit rider with a good seat, whose reins hand is at once confident and sympathetic, will be the master who will get the best out of his polo pony.

STOPPING AND TURNING

The polo pony is being asked constantly to stop and turn or pull up and then go promptly into a gallop from a near standstill. As the horseman knows, his mount is stopped by bringing its hocks under its belly – transferring its weight from its forelegs to its hindlegs and making it lift its head. The rider achieves this not by yanking on the reins or tugging at the animal's head but by squeezing hard with both legs close to the girth and feeling on the reins.

A well schooled polo pony is one, too, which can turn tightly, which means turning, collected, on the hocks. As the horseman knows, for a turn to the left pressure is applied with the right leg, the left leg eased away. In turning to the right the leg aids are reversed.

RIDING OFF

The subject of riding off was introduced in Chapter One. Since it is assumed that the beginner's pony is a well schooled one it is also taken that it will go obediently and fearlessly into the ride off.

The player rides off to take his opposite number away from the ball, to prevent himself being pushed over the line, or to push an opponent, in possession of the ball, over the line and have it for himself. This being a principal and integral polo action, it should be frequently practised.

The art of riding off lies in applying the outer leg hard and throwing the pony's weight against the opponent's pony, at a narrow angle – to give the pony the superior advantage – the knee in front of the opponent's knees. Keeping his elbow against his ribs the player then leans out of the saddle and drives the point of his shoulder into his opponent's side.

STICKS

Guided by personal experiment and the advice of his instructor the player will buy sticks with handles and heads, and of lengths, that suit him best. He will probably start with a longer stick than he will use when his style becomes more elastic. The longer the stick the greater the velocity and length he should get on his shots and the longer the reach he will have. If he owns ponies of different heights he will perhaps require sticks to suit each. Before even starting to swing a stick, the beginner will be shown by his instructor how to grip, and how to use its grip loop.

When he starts practice games he will, as a contingency against breakage, keep a spare stick or two on the side of the ground.

THE POLO STROKES

It is a truism – mentioned in Chapter One, but worth repeating here – that the person who will emerge most readily as a polo player is not so much the one who is only an outstanding natural horseman – however much that may help – as the one who is a natural ball-game player, a cricketer, hockey, racquets or tennis player. Given sufficient enthusiasm, however, coupled with a great deal of intelligent practice and stick-and-ball sense, a good style can be developed. (By the same token a brilliant all-round ball-game player, who has never been near a horse, should be able to learn to ride for polo reasonably quickly, if he becomes fond of polo ponies and works hard and faithfully at the equestrian precepts. In fact it is more difficult to teach a non-ball-game player who is an experienced horseman to strike a ball effectively than it is to teach a natural ball-game player to ride.)

There are four principal polo strokes and eight subsidiary strokes. The basic strokes are the offside forehander (the most used), the offside backhander, the nearside forehander and the nearside backhander.

The subsidiary strokes, which are pulled, cut or flicked, are the nearside and offside under-the-neck shots, the nearside and offside under-the-tail shots (pulled), the offside and nearside forehand cuts and the offside and nearside backhand cuts.

The beginner will be concerned for some time only with the four fundamental strokes. He should avoid the temptation of devoting too much time to the easiest stroke which is the offside forehander. Accomplishment of the others will be almost as important to him.

The aim will be to strike the ball with the centre of the stick head with sufficient impetus to carry it the desired distance, and the control to take it in the right direction time and again.

The instructor, while urging him to focus his attention unswervingly on the ball will show him the correct swing and timing, how to drive a ball and how to loft it.

A ball driven along the ground will clearly gain less velocity, length and accuracy than one that is lofted clear and free. The most effective point of impact being below the ball's equator, therefore, the swing should bring the stick head close to the ground. This will be doubly important on a rough or badly cut-up ground.

INITIAL LESSONS IN THE STROKES

For convenience, in order to enjoy a perfectly still stance or seat while concentrating entirely on the lessons in hand, and also to avoid damaging a pony's legs, the beginner will probably start to learn his strokes standing on a chair, chest, or packing case, or whatever, then proceeding to the polo pit's wooden horse.

A properly appointed polo pit should have a sloping floor surrounding a flat centre on which the wooden horse stands – complete with saddle, stirrups and a rein. The high wire-mesh walls protrude inwards near the bottom to prevent hard-hit balls climbing them. When the ball is hit it travels up the slope, is stopped by the protruding net and rolls back towards the striker. He thus gains practice from a riding position at hitting a moving ball, without having to attend to a pony.

He will particularly bear in mind at this stage that every stroke is made off his feet, not off his saddle, and – aware that he will normally be taking his shots at speed – that he should keep his weight well over the front of the saddle. He will avoid the pernicious habit of simply clouting the ball indiscriminately, but will always aim it, accurate passing and goal shooting being an essential element of the strike in team play.

As soon as he is reasonably confident, from dummy practice, that he is closely familiar with (if not the complete master of) the four main strokes, he should attempt them from a pony. As soon as possible, he should be practicing from the polo-match reality of a gallop.

Stick-and-ball is most usefully practiced with another player. It gives the advantage of trying out the strokes on a moving ball and also the chance to practice riding off.

But none of that is to say he will not return for more practice in the pit to improve his swing, follow-through, style and accuracy. By now he will have attempted the under-the-neck and under-the-tail shots and the various cut shots to the side. In all these things he will follow his instructor's advice.

WATCHING GOOD PLAY, THE GAME'S NEXT-TO-BEST TUTOR

As his practical education proceeds the novice will endeavour to watch as much good (high- or medium-goal) polo as he is able to, preferably with the bird's-eye view advantage of a seat high up on the stands. He should be in the company, if he can, of a veteran who can interpret the play for him, criticising or applauding as may be, each chukka, and explaining the fouls and penalty awards. Watching high-class play probably is the next best tutor of the game to personal involvement. (And can be of much greater benefit than personal involvement.)

Let us imagine the novice player sitting up there with his mentor. An umpire has thrown the ball between the Greens and the Whites and the game is opening up. The respective team members are no longer in direct rivalry with their corresponding numbers as they were at the line-up, but are marking their opposite numbers, the *Ones* versus the *Backs* – the *Twos* against the *Threes*.

The White *Three* has the ball – unmarked for the moment and at a good gallop – but is ridden over the line by the Green *Two*. The Greens are attacking, The Green *Two*'s stick is hooked and he loses the ball, but he is well covered by his Number *Three*, who is quickly in possession. He passes it up to his Number *One*, who has positioned himself well up the ground to receive it. The Number *One* takes it on, hotly pursued by the White *Back*. Just as the Number *One* thinks himself to be within two more easy shots of the glory of a goal, however, he hears a shout from behind 'Man!'

Unhesitatingly he aims his pony in a little and when the White *Back* is level he leans his pony's weight into him – with his knee in front of the opponent's knee – and rides him to the side. That leaves the Green

Three, who is a very accurate striker, an apparently unhindered path to the White goal. However, the White *Two*, who is on a very fast pony, is now catching him up. He attempts to ride him off, but, in doing so, gallops in front of him. The whistle blows, the game is stopped, a penalty is awarded against the Whites. The Greens score from the 40-yard mark ... And while the teams change ends and line up in the centre of the ground, up in the stands the tyro listens to his mentor.

THE ROLES

This subject has been introduced in Chapter One under the sub-heading *Team Positions*. The novice will begin his game career either at *Back* which is, if anything, the easiest place to fill. Or at Number *One*, which can on no account be called 'the easiest', although it is the one in which most beginners find themselves – since *Back* is a position favoured by players with longer experience, players, too, who are particularly reliable with backhand shots.

Wherever he starts (in order to gain a useful grasp of the whole game) the novice must set out to absorb a close knowledge of the roles and duties of all four positions.

NUMBER ONE

The Number *One* is the team's front attacker. Being marked in attack by the opposing *Back*, he must try to elude him, keep well up the pitch to take passes and, whenever the opportunity occurs, go for a goal. In different tactical circumstances it may be his turn to push the opposing *Back* away from the goalmouth and make openings for his Number *Two* or Number *Three*, who will almost certainly be stronger players than himself.

In defence the Number *One*'s task is to mark the opposing *Back* as closely and positively as can be.

There will be times when he will interchange with the other forward, the Number *Two*.

The Number *One* should be a lightweight and ride the fastest and handiest possible ponies. It is essential that he be an accurate striker of the ball. To that end, out of the game a regular Number *One* should frequently practice shooting at goal from difficult angles.

NUMBER TWO

The Number *Two*, the senior of the forwards, marks the opposing Number *Three*, who is likely to be the strongest and best mounted man in the opponents' line-up.

The Number *Two* should be the one most likely to develop his team's attacks. On average he should be scoring most of his squad's goals. He must be well mounted, a really hard worker, a long hitter and a marksman at top pace. Practicing at stick-and-ball he should put in a lot of time improving his accuracy with goal-shots.

He and his Number *One* should have a close mutual understanding and plan of action. Their positions are essentially interchangeable. In possession of the ball the Number *Two* has to decide in what circumstances to pass it to his Number *One* and when to take it on himself. Sometimes this is obvious. If the Number *Two* is too well marked for comfort and about to lose possession of the ball, he should probably pass it up. If, on the other hand, the Number *One* is successfully marking the opposing *Back* the Number *Two*, if not too closely challenged, will head straight for goal himself.

NUMBER THREE

The Number *Three*, being the team pivot, and half-back, the link between the forwards and *Back*, is in the best position to be the captain, too. Having to be equally energetic and responsible in attack and defence, he must be a really capable striker all round his pony – and also a long one – and should be as well mounted as can be.

It will rest chiefly on the shoulders of the Number *Three* to turn defence into attack. His primary task is then to send well-aimed passes up to his forwards (in particular to the Number *One*), passes that can be readily intercepted before an opponent can reach them, passes driven in front of the forward. Just because the *Three* is the strongest team member it is not his business selfishly to retain the ball and go for goal himself, unless his forwards have altogether failed to keep their positions or unless they are closely marked and he is loose. On the other hand he must press the attack, supporting and covering his forwards, being ready to take up the ball if they lose it.

He must, at the same time, be ready to turn sharply to stop the opposing *Two* – his opposite number – if that man gains possession.

In defence the Number *Three* will cover his *Back* and contain the enemy *Two*.

The best Number *Three*, a really dynamic pivot – like an outstanding leader in any other sphere – will make his fellow team-members feel and perform at the top of their capacity.

BACK

Dependability should be the *Back*'s chief characteristic. He must be a long and reliable hitter with a special facility for effective backhanders, in terms both of length and accuracy. (Clearly it is much safer for him to gallop back and use his backhanders than to attempt to meet the ball head on.)

His primary responsibility is to prevent the opposition scoring, his particular duty being to mark and obstruct the Opposing *One* or the first man through in attack. He will cover his Number *Three* and be ready to take the ball if the *Three* misses.

In attack the *Back* should endeavour to pass to his Number *Two*. He will keep up the ground in a close supportive role, but will not allow the opposing Number *One* to give him the slip.

THE ALL-ROUNDER

A good team player is one who is sufficiently confident and knowledge-able to read and interpret the whole game at every moment of play. Therefore the sooner he pushes to be allowed to play in each of the four positions the better. By that means he should develop a strong 'polo sense', the vital sense of anticipation which helps to give the instinctive facility of being in the right place at the right time.

The sooner, too, that he starts umpiring modest club games the better it will be for his tactical understanding of polo and thus for his own improvement. But that is looking far ahead.

THE CAPTAIN

Whether in the *Three* slot, or in another position, it is the captain's responsibility to brief his team on general tactical policy; to appraise the opposition's performance as well as that of his own squad, chukka by chukka; to guide and criticise as necessary between chukkas or at half-time; to give praise where praise is due; to keep high the team's morale; to insist on their punctuality, proper dress and tack and the due attentiveness of their grooms; and to ensure that spare sticks have been arranged. The captain may have much closer responsibility than all this, depending upon the team's circumstances.

A good captain will know his men, their strengths, their short-comings and also, if possible, the respective qualities of their ponies.

CALLS

Most players will agree that the less shouting there is on the ground the better, and that includes orders from the captain. But some terse orders are valid, and the beginner in the Number *One* position will soon become accustomed to the following injunctions being hurled at his back:

'Leave it!'

'Man!' Brief for 'Ride your man!' It means that a team-mate behind believes that there is more chance of success if the one in front takes care of the opposition while he goes through with the ball.

'Go!' Meaning 'leave the ball to me and continue up the field either to take my pass or ride off any opponent who may try to intercept me.'

'Ball!' or 'Take it!' Meaning 'Have a go, I'm covering you in case you miss.'

'Turn!' 'Turn up!' or 'Turn back!' Given when an opponent's back-hander is about to be hit; when play has changed, or is about to change direction. It is generally directed at a player who has failed to anticipate this.

HOOKING (see pp 20, 21)

It is no exaggeration to say that, whenever the opportunity occurs to hook the stick of an opponent in possession of the ball it should be taken.

TEMPER AND EQUANIMITY

Since the more experienced players are inclined to become heated and excited in the tumult of the chukka, especially when things are going wrong, they will often get vociferously angry with the performances (or lack of them) from newcomers to the game.

The beginner is likely to endure much abuse, and he will simply have to learn not to allow such bouts of ill-temper to spoil his enjoyment of the game. If he does not understand what crime he has committed (it is difficult to take in all but the briefest of injunctions during play) he is entitled to a proper explanation from the indignant one at the end of the chukka, or after the match.

BASIC TACTICS

To sum up the tasks of the *One* and *Two*, when on the attack they are to keep well forward, hinder the opposition and shoot goals. In defence they are to mark, to obstruct – or steer away from the goalmouth – and take the ball from the *Three* and *Back* or to hinder their shots. The jobs of the *Three* and *Back* are to create opportunities for the forwards by sending them well-placed passes, and to support them in the offensive; and, of the *Three* in particular, to take over the spearhead role if necessary. In defence they are to mark their opposite numbers and to prevent them from getting within striking distance of their own goal; and to turn defence into attack.

There are two reliable ways of scoring goals; one involves *taking* the ball up the ground by skilled tactics; the other involves *sending* it up by skilled tactics. Good polo tactics are based on line-ahead passing, not on clever and prolonged individual ball control, dribbling and circling – spectacular as all that may look from the stands, and effective as it unfortunately often is when the game is dominated, or almost dominated, by one man.

The golden words which should be imprinted on the tyro's mind are BALL CONTROL – ANTICIPATION – PACE. *Be unmarked in attack. When the game turns, take the nearest man, ball or no ball.*

HIT OUT FROM BEHIND (see p. 23)

This will be taken by the *Back* or *Three*, depending probably upon which of them is the longest and most accurate striker. He will aim the ball to the player whom he believes to be the one who will get away with it most effectively, and who is least closely marked. His team-mates will position themselves according to a pre-arranged deployment.

The opponents will endeavour to elude their opposite numbers. As the opposing *Back* or *Three* is about to hit the ball they should begin to rein forward, rather than awaiting the ball at a standstill. Their aim will be to meet the ball without crossing the line of it.

PENALTY HITS (see p. 22)

In the case of the *Back* taking a 60-yarder, his *Forwards* will place themselves on the back line, either side of the goalmouth, the Number *Three* about 20 yards in – in line with the left goal post. The defenders will mark their opposite numbers, but must keep a minimum of 30 yards from the ball.

In the case of the Number *Three* taking a 30- or 40-yarder – when the defending team may not cross the back line before the ball is struck – the *Forwards* will deploy on his flanks, with the *Back* covering him behind. The moment the ball is struck the defenders will follow out in an endeavour to intercept according to a pre-planned drill.

FREE HIT (see p. 22)

Given from the spot where the foul took place; none of the side fouling to be within 30 yards of the ball; the side fouled to go where they choose. Supposing the hit is taken by the *Back*, he should probably send it to his *Three* or *Two* while the *One* gallops ahead, anticipating a pass.

FOULS (see pp. 19–22)

The tyro, having thoroughly acquainted himself with the rules will have an academic knowledge of what constitutes fouling. He is bound to learn much more once he starts in the hurly-burly of chukkas, and painfully, too – from the discipline of the umpire's whistle. Fouls – apart from slowing up the game – are dangerous to pony and player and must be vigilantly avoided.

'Dangerous riding' is an infringement that should incur a penalty. 'Crossing' is also 'dangerous riding'. Although the crossing rules and their safeguards were outlined in Chapter One it may as well be repeated here that to rob an opponent of the ball, the player either hooks his stick, rides him off the line, or overtakes him and reaches the line so far ahead as not to endanger him or his pony. Two players reaching the line of the ball simultaneously from opposite directions must both go for the shot on the offside.

Crosses from the hit out from the back line are all too easily committed by both sides.

Appealing for fouls is bad sportsmanship and bad polo.

In the case of a player bringing on a pony that plays up to the extent that it imperils other ponies and players, he should be instructed to remove it from the ground and exchange it.

IN GENERAL

From the time he is first a spectator the polo aspirant should be envisaging the tactical structure of the game, becoming a better critic and shrewd interpreter of the development of each match. That is a habit which will help enormously when he is playing. It will make it that much simpler for him to have in his mind a bird's-eye view of his own game, to dovetail his own actions with those of the rest of his team, to think the essential two strokes ahead and take quick decisions that brook not one second's delay, decisions such as which way to pass, when to turn, when to interchange positions, when to take the man rather than the ball.

As in any other team game unselfishness is an essential criterion. The best polo matches are won by interplay; by passing the ball, not dribbling and conjuring with it; by team effort, not by solo display. And here are two more good principles: a player who is doing nothing is doing wrong; and, secondly, there should never be more than two players on the same side in a mêlée, but always one forward and one back.

Of course much more could be written of polo tactics. But the purpose of this guide is only to indicate to someone who is thinking of taking up polo what is in store for him or her in the early days. Besides which tactics are much better taught by visual demonstration.

PHYSICAL FITNESS

No branch of equestrian sport demands greater stamina than polo. The beginner is therefore advised to aim towards a peak of physical fitness at the outset of his career in the game. Being 'riding fit' demands a great deal of riding. Being fit for polo, however, is achieved not only by riding but by indulging in every other form of hard exercise available to the player, tennis, squash, swimming, jogging, etc. And, of course, by observing all the fundamental tenets of good health. He should practise all the equestrian loosening up and strengthening exercises set by his instructor – with a will. The more weight he loses, too, the better it will be for his ponies!

IN THE RIGHT SPIRIT

With its macho-glamorous image polo has become something of a status symbol, and too many beginners, in recent years, have taken up the game with a false approach. The Hurlingham Polo Association's 1988 handbook suggests most succinctly the attitude of certain tyros: 'A lot of them remain at very low handicaps, and one wonders whether the motive is to play polo or to put a pair of boots on, and a Lock hat in the back window of the Porsche!' Suffice to say that the polo world does not welcome people of bogus intent into its fraternity. The game should be taken up for its own sake only.

START WELL, START YOUNG

No parent in Britain whose young son or daughter is keen on both sport and ponies should miss the opportunity of enlisting them with their local branch of the Pony Club – with a view to starting them in polo in their growing years. Or, if their local branch is not into polo, let them find the nearest and best that is. For it is an inestimable advantage to make a start in any game in childhood and none more so than in polo. The well-known English polo names – Hipwood, Kent, Horswell, Elliott, Harper, Hine, Livingstone-Learmonth, Williams, Seavill, Matthews, Brodie, Waddington and Tylor – are testimony enough to the advantage of the Pony Club. Those all began their careers there.

Any parent who is in doubt regarding the merits of Pony Club polo should witness the generously sponsored annual championships which attract over 60 team entries and which – following preliminary matches at several different clubs – culminate in a jamboree of finals at Cowdray Park, Sussex. There the under-21s compete for the Jack Gannon trophy, the under-19s for the main prize, the Rendell Cup, the under-16s for the Loriners trophy and the under-14s for the Handley Cross cup. Parents should see, too, the championships' camp in the

Plate 9 (*above*) A close challenge for the ball during the final of the 1986 Warwickshire Cup, at Cirencester Park, Gloucestershire. (*left to right*) Jesus Baez of Mexico (handicap 6), Alan Kent (GB, 6), Martin Brown (GB, 6) and Owen Rinehart (USA, 9).

(*below*) A 40-yard penalty shot.

Plate 10   (*above*) Turning the play: (*left to right*) Gabriel Donoso (Chile, 8), Martin Glue (GB, 5), Howard Hipwood (GB, 9), Alan Kent (GB, 7) and John Yeoman (GB, 3).

(*below*) Action during the 1982 match for the Coronation Cup. The British players Alan Kent (*middle*), flanked by Julian Hipwood (*left*) and Howard Hipwood (*right*) are galloping back, attempting to prevent a New Zealand goal.

Plate 11
In the pony lines.

The champion pony,
Spice, the property of
Galen Weston of
Canada.

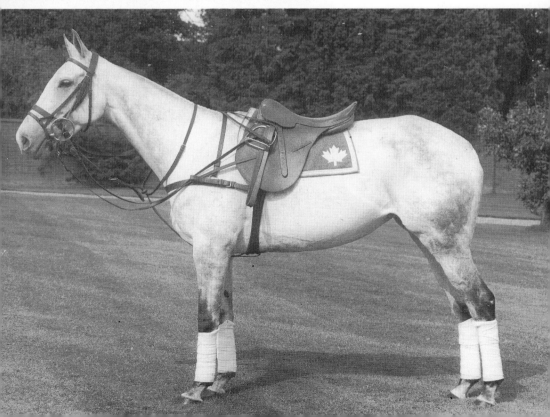

Plate 12
Under instruction:
(*above*) Mr Somerville
Livingstone-Learmonth
with one of his pupils.
(*right*) A player
practising shots from a
wooden horse.

Plate 13   Race for the ball.

Plate 14 Starting young: children at play during the Pony Club Championships.

Plate 15 (*above*) How starting young pays off. Julian Hipwood, captain of the 1962 winning Pony Club team receiving his prize from Colonel the Hon. Guy Cubitt, founder of Britain's Pony Club. Howard Hipwood stands to the left of Julian. They have been Britain's two leading players throughout the 1980s. (*below*) Harry Payne Whitney leading the American champions, who came to be known as 'The Big Four'. The other three are Devereux Milburn and Monty and Larry Waterbury. They won the Westchester Cup in 1909 and 1911. The sculptor was Herbert Haseltine.

Plate 16   (*above, left*) The great Tommy Hitchcock Jnr. (*above, right*) Stewart Iglehart, a member of the American 1936 Westchester team. He was also a scratch golfer and leading ice hockey player. (*below*) The world's top woman player, Claire Tomlinson of England, with her pony, Queenie. Mrs Tomlinson is a 4-goaler.

evenings with its happy revelry amid the caravans, tents, stabling, horse boxes and trailers. The event has always been run with the greatest good order and efficiency combined with a wonderful aura of camaraderie.

Players rising to the Gannon category, which involves 4-chukka matches, require two ponies, but until then a boy or girl needs only one, which may cost well under £1,000 in Britain.

The Hurlingham Polo Association subsidise the award of Pony Club scholarships, of which there are several each year to New Zealand, Argentina and Brazil. The Whitfield Court Polo school in Ireland and the Rangitiki, in Berkshire, have also allotted free places to some of those among the most promising young players.

4

THE HERITAGE

IN ANCIENT PERSIA

Since the first records of a mounted ball game emanate from the Persia of some 2,500 years ago we may assume that the cradle of what would become the highly sophisticated game of modern polo were the lands that bestrode the rivers Tigris and Euphrates. Known then as *chaugán*, a mallet, it was essentially a royal and aristocratic sport and one expressly designed to promote equestrian and cavalry skills. Sometimes played with six-a-side, sometimes eight, sometimes many more, the Persian game was heralded, and played, amid a good deal of noisy ceremony. Here is the poet Firdusi in *The Book of Kings* (AD 1010): 'Then the band began to play and the air was filled with dust. You would have thought there was an earthquake so great was the noise of trumpets and cymbals. Then the king started the game by throwing in the ball in the correct manner.'

Firdusi took much poetic licence in his writings on polo. Describing a match between seven Persians and seven Turks, he states that the Persian Siáwasch, the country's leading player, struck the ball so hard that 'it almost reaches the moon', while another star performer, Gushtasp, wields his *chaugán* with such force that 'the ball could no longer be seen by any person on the maidá [plain], as his blow had caused it to vanish amongst the clouds'. The historian Cinnanus shows Comnenus (Alexius I, Byzantine emperor, 1048–1118) enjoying *chaugán* with his courtiers, and adds: 'This is the game then, a very doubtful and dangerous one, as he who would play it must be constantly lying flat on his horse, and bending himself on either side, and be turning his horse very sharply, and he must manage to ride, so as to be skilled in moving his body and his horse in as many different ways as the ball is driven.' Another Persian poet, Nizam of Ganja (AD 1140–1202) recounts how

50

the beautiful Shírin, Queen of Khusran Parviz the Victorious, played *chaugán* with her ladies-in-waiting against the King and his courtiers:

> *On one side was the Moon and her Stars*
> *On the other the Shah and his Firman Bearers*

IN MOGUL INDIA

During the reign of Queen Elizabeth I, the three Sherley brothers travelling in India and visiting the court of Akbar (1542–1602), witnessed that greatest of the Mogul emperors at play. 'There were twelve horsemen,' the Sherleys' secretary, George Manwaring wrote: 'so they divided themselves, six on one side, six on the other, having in their hands long rods of wood about the bigness of a man's finger, and at one end of the rods a piece of wood nailed like a hammer. After they were divided and turned face to face, there came one in the middle and threw a ball between the companies and, having goals made at either end of the plain, they began their sport, striking the ball with their rods one to the other in the fashion of our football here in England.'

IN THE FAR EAST

From Persia and other parts of the near East the game was introduced into China and Japan, where it was known as *daiku*, meaning 'Strike the ball'. Polo almost died out in Japan during the nineteenth-century rebellion that ended the feudal system, but, by the 1880s it was revived. Its career in China continued unbroken and from there it went to Tibet, where it was known as *pulu*, the Tibetan word for a ball.

THE MANIPURIS

It was almost certainly from Tibet that the people of Manipur – that mountainous state sandwiched between Assam and Burma – adopted the game. The Manipuris called it *kán-jāi-bazèè*, but they knew it, too, as *pulu*, the word that so comfortably adapted to make our title for the game.

Many of the Manipuri villages established their simple polo clubs, and during the 1850s and after these were joined by some of the European tea planters. Lieutenant Joseph Sherer, a subaltern in the Bengal Army, played his first game with the Manipuris in 1854. After the Indian Mutiny, he and his friend Captain Robert Stewart, Superintendent of Cachar, founded the first European polo club in Manipur in 1859.

Joe Sherer (who was to be a major-general) wrote: 'The Manipooris were no respecter of persons. It was quite permissible, and recognised as lawful, to ride *at*, and *through* anything or anybody that came between the player and the spot where the ball lay. I was once caught in this position ... and was simply sent spinning, pony and all, and got considerably shaken and bruised.' Polo continued to be played, as it had been played for so long in old Manipur, in many remote corners of India at least until the Second World War.

THE BIRTH OF MODERN POLO

Considering the germ of the Manipuris' game entered the British *raj* during the 1850s and then spread rapidly through the Army of India, it is perhaps surprising that polo's introduction into the Western world was not directly to England via regiments lately stationed in that sub-continent.

What in fact happened was that in 1869 officers of the 10th Hussars, camping at Aldershot that summer and being impressed by an account of the Manipuris' game in *The Field*, sent for their chargers, fashioned some sticks and a ball and began knocking it about in imitation of the magazine's description. They then acquired some 13–14 hh ponies from Ireland and organised friendly matches between themselves. They called it 'Hockey on Horseback'. The number of players on each side was according to whim. Eight-a-side seems to have been the popular number. The first inter-regimental challenge was between the 10th Hussars and 9th Lancers that autumn.

JOHN WATSON

In 1872 the 10th Hussars were posted to India, being followed there a few years later by the 9th Lancers, and the game, which they had developed in England, soon superseded the rough-and-tumble sport which the Manipuris had shown the British *Raj*. The outstanding player of those early years was Captain John Watson of the 13th Hussars. The son of Robert Watson, a famous Irish sportsman and Master of Foxhounds, John Watson was the first man to demonstrate the usefulness of the backhand shots which he had practised assiduously.

When Lord Roberts took command of the Madras army he recognised at once what an import element in army life polo had become. But it was obvious to him that the play was too loose and the rules too haphazard. John Watson was the officer whom Roberts selected to recommend future guidelines for the safety and discipline of the game.

Polo in India, where the game could be played the whole year round, added immensely to its vigour and standard at home. Owing largely to the encouragement given to the Army and the much easier economic situation, the game was far more generally available there.

THE HURLINGHAM CLUB AND THE RISING POPULARITY

Founded in 1873, London's Hurlingham was the first polo club in the Western world. Among its rules, which became universal, were a pony height limit of 14 hands; no more than five players allowed on each side; the goals to be at least 250 yards apart; the goalposts to be eight yards apart; the ball to be three inches in diameter; and an offside rule. 'A player may interpose his pony before his antagonist, so as to prevent the latter reaching the ball, whether in full career or otherwise,' the club also stipulated, 'but may not cross another player, in possession of the ball, unless at such a distance as to avoid all possibility of a collision . . . It is allowed to hook an adversary's stick, but neither under nor over an adversary's pony.'

The Hurlingham was followed by four more London clubs, the Roehampton, the Ranelagh, the Eden Park and the London. In Britain as a whole before the end of the century there were nearly 70 clubs and over 1,000 players. The game was nowhere stronger – with the exception of India – than in Ireland.

Winston Churchill gives some idea of the universal importance of the game in India in his autobiographical *My Early Life*. He describes how he and two brother-officers in the 4th Hussars pooled their resources and '. . . thus freed from mundane cares devoted themselves to the serious purpose of life. This was expressed in the one word – POLO. It was upon this, apart from duty, that all our interest was concentrated.'

EXPORTED TO THE USA

James Gordon Bennett, Editor-in-Chief of the *New York Herald* – the journalist who, among several other enterprises, sent H. M. Stanley to find Dr Livingstone in 1871 – was also the man instrumental in starting polo in the United States. Enormously impressed by what he saw of the game at Hurlingham in 1876, Bennett returned to the States with a plentiful supply of sticks and balls, sent to Texas for some suitable ponies and staged a demonstration game in New York, in 'Old Dickel's Indoor Riding Academy' – strictly according to the Hurlingham rules.

In 1879 the Long Island club, which was to be known two years later as the Meadow Brook, started up. Then the Queen's County and Brighton clubs were founded, with August Belmont, H. L. Herbert, W. A. Hazard and Tommy Hitchcock Snr as the next great pioneering names.

THE WESTCHESTER CUP

A whole decade went by before Hurlingham discovered that the game was well underway in America. Griswold Lorillard, of the Westchester club, having informed his surprised Hurlingham hosts at a dinner in the spring of 1886, promptly invited an all-England team to compete on Rhode Island that summer for a cup to be known as 'the Westchester'. The Hurlingham team, under the captaincy of the pre-eminent John Watson was completed by Captains the Hon. Richard Lawley and Thomas Hone, both of the 7th Hussars, and Malcolm Little, 9th Lancers, accompanied by their ponies. Their opponents were Thomas Hitchcock (Snr), Raymond Belmont, Foxhall P. Keene and W. K. Thorn. In a series of matches, each of three long chukkas, England came through as decisive victors.

The United States Polo Association then set to work improving their individual play, their team tactics and the schooling of their ponies, and, in 1902, threw down the gauntlet for another Westchester challenge. This time, with the Nickalls brothers, Walter Buckmaster, Frederick Freake and C. D. Miller representing England, and Foxhall Keene, John Cowdin, Rodolphe Agassiz and the Waterbury brothers, Monty and Larry, sharing the chukkas for America, the return contest was played at Hurlingham. In a best of three, each of six 10-minute chukkas, the Americans won the first match, 2–1, but then, losing 6–1 and 7–1, failed to take the cup home.

In 1909 the forceful American captain Harry Payne Whitney, who had been busy improving his country's polo, decided the time had really come to take the Westchester back to the States. His team was completed by Devereux Milburn, a brilliant Back, and the Waterbury brothers as forwards. Competing at Hurlingham in June and July those players, who were to be famous as 'the Big Four', won outright, 9–5 and 8–2.

America won again in 1911 and 1913, but lost to Hurlingham in 1914. The American squad was composed that year of Monty and Larry Waterbury, Devereux Milburn and René La Montagne, the English of Leslie Cheape, Vivian Lockett, 'Rattle' Barrett and H. A. Tomkinson.

THE FIRST 10-GOALERS

In 1891 the Americans introduced the handicapping system, and between then and 1914 the following 10-goal ratings were awarded. From the USA, Foxhall Keene, Rodolphe Agazziz, Thomas Hitchcock (Snr) and the Waterbury brothers. From England: 'Rattle' Barrett, Leslie Cheape, E. W. E. Palmes, R. G. Ritson, Walter Buckmaster, J. Hardress Lloyd, Vivian Lockett and Lord Wodehouse.

AMERICA CHANGES THE RULES

The British, the originators of polo, had a maximum height rules for ponies, which had been revised in the 1880s, from 14 hh to 14.2 hh. The Americans abolished that rule thereby more or less cancelling out Britain's great advantage in native mountain and moorland breeds. Meanwhile the offside rule had also been done away with, which radically altered the tactics of the game.

The Westchester Cup was contested again in 1921, 1924, 1927, 1930, 1936, and 1939. The United States won on every occasion. Tommy Hitchcock (Jnr) was the great star, other big American names being Devereux Milburn, Malcolm Stevenson, Watson Webb, Mike Phipps, Eric Pedley, Winston Guest and Stewart Iglehart. Among the top English players between the wars were Vivian Lockett, H. A. Tomkinson, 'Rattle' Barrett, E. G. Atkinson, Hesketh Hughes, David Dawnay, Claud Pert, Humphrey Guinness, Eric Tyrell-Martin and Gerald Balding.

POLO SPREADS AROUND THE WORLD

British ranchers in the Argentine were soon playing polo, a Mr Shennan being the first in 1877. By the end of the 1880s three clubs, including the renowned Hurlingham, were firmly established around Buenos Aires. The Anglo-Argentinian Traills were the best known polo family there; of those Johnny Traill was the principal star. The English pony breeds, crossed with the local *estancia* ponies, the *criollos*, and schooled on cattle, made very handy mounts.

Promoted by Englishmen and Americans, polo was also played by the turn of the century in Chile, Uruguay, Colombia and Brazil.

From the Malta club (founded 1874) the Royal Navy carried polo to New Zealand, Gibraltar, Tangier, Tunis, Bizerta, Algiers, Crete, Egypt, Rome, Cannes, Madrid, Barcelona, Salonika, Constantinople and the China station. New Zealand's initial demonstration of the game, by British naval officers, was in 1888. The country's premier tournament for the Savile Cup was first challenged in 1890. By 1930 there were 16 clubs in New Zealand. Australia's polo birth was even earlier than New Zealand's, the game being first shown there by the St Quinton brothers in 1876. The Australian 'Waler' (New South Wales) pony was soon to improve the stock in India.

Australian polo was to be closely connected with cattle and sheep farming. Four sheep-raising brothers called Ashton took their country's game onto the international stage in the 1930s when they hired a small boat, in which they sailed themselves and their ponies to England and reached the final at Hurlingham. Changing ship they went on to New York, won most of their matches there, too, and then sold their ponies to a number of millionaires for $77,000.

In 1938, Australia's first 10-goaler emerged – Bob Skene.

In the 1870s and '80s, clubs were formed in France, Italy, Hungary, Poland and Austria. The game was first played in South Africa between British regiments in 1875; it began in Ghana in 1902; in Kenya in 1903 and in Nigeria in 1904.

Some of the world's best players between the wars were to be found in India, either among the native aristocracy – the best of whom was Rao Rajah Hanut Singh – or in the Indian Army. In 1927 the Westchester team was drawn entirely from the Indian Army, the representative names being Atkinson, Dening, George, Pert, Roark and Williams.

While many rich, athletic young Indians fielded private teams, the officers of each of the cavalry regiments stationed there had 500 troop horses of a handy 15.0–15.3 hands to choose from. The infantry battalions also maintained a good nucleus of horses and many of their officers played on their pay.

Indian polo was immortalised by Rudyard Kipling in *The Maltese Cat*, the game's first literary classic. It is an anthropomorphic tale of the inter-regimental final between the smart, expensively mounted Archangels and the Skidars ('what they call a pioneer regiment'), the leading light of whose stables was 'the Cat', and through whose eyes Kipling tells the story.

With war looming in the late 1930s the great days of polo in India closed, never to return.

THE ARGENTINE ASCENDANCY

The Argentines, being nationally athletic and adept at ball games and having the gift of the ranch pony, polo was booming in their country by the time of the First World War, although neither Britain nor the United States took Argentina's national standard seriously until the 1920s. The international agreement to raise the embargo on the pony height limit posed no problem in Argentina. They had a vast fund of ponies, and, crossing some of the best of their ranch mares with English Thoroughbreds, they were soon producing the best in the world.

In 1922 the team sent to England by the Jockey Club of Buenos Aires beat all their challengers (except the regimental champions, the 17th Lancers, who were captained by the great Colonel Vivian Lockett). Thereupon the United States Polo Association invited the same team (drawn from Juan and Luis Nelson, Luis Lacey and Juan and David Miles) to take part in the American national championships, and the Argentines won.

They went on to try their hand against the American national squad (Tommy Hitchcock, Devereux Milburn, Watson Webb and Louis Stoddard) to whom they lost. But they defeated them in the 1920 Paris Olympics. In 1932 the Copa de las Americas – expressly instituted for matches between the USA and the Argentine – was challenged for the first time. The Americans secured it on that occasion, but never again.

The Argentines went on to be polo champions at the 1936 Berlin Olympics and have proved more or less invincible ever since.

It was not long before Argentina could stage an exhibition match between two 40-goal teams. Today she lists 150 clubs, supporting over 5,000 players.

LATTER-DAY AMERICAN POLO

American polo suffered little from the Second World War except that the great Thomas Hitchcock Jnr was killed – while commanding a fighter squadron – in a flying accident in England in 1944.

Long Island, the old cradle of American polo became so developed after the war that the orientation transferred to New York and thence to Oak Brook, near Chicago. Texas, under the inspiration of the Barry family also became a great centre, and so did Florida under the Beveridge brothers, who took over the Gulf Stream Club from Mike Phipps and Stewart Iglehart, and who started up the Boca Raton Club between Miami and Palm Beach. In the 1970s William T. Ylvisaker, founder of the Polo Training Foundation, established the Palm Beach Polo and Country Club, where the World Cup is staged.

By the late 1970s the United States counted 120 clubs with 2,500 names on the handicap lists. Before the end of the 1980s that figure was nearer 10,000.

POST-WAR REVIVAL IN ENGLAND

Most of the English county clubs got going again with slow chukkas soon after the war ended, but all the old London clubs, which had closed in 1939, failed to revive, with the exception of the Roehampton where polo was kept going until its eclipse in 1952.

The man who got England back onto the international stage was Lord Cowdray, whose father, the 2nd Viscount, had laid down his pioneer grounds at Cowdray Park before the First World War. The 3rd Viscount was non-playing captain of the English Westchester team in 1939. He lost an arm with the BEF in France in 1940 yet continued to play regularly until the 1960s.

It was this Viscount Cowdray who, in 1949, invited Juan (Jack) Nelson and Luis Lalor to bring a few ponies for sale and watch some of the best polo that Britain could then exhibit. Duly impressed, the

Argentinians suggested to him that he might escort an all-England team to play in their country that autumn. Lord Cowdray took his brother-in-law, John Lakin, Lt-Col Humphrey Guinness, John Traill Jnr, Lt-Col Peter Dollar and Bob Skene. The team drawn from that party defeated Chile and, indeed, did very well throughout the tour.

In 1951 Lord Cowdray invited his Argentine hosts to send a medium-goal team to Cowdray Park. Lakin, Guinness, Gerald Balding and Lt-Col A. F. Harper (since Hon. Secretary of the Hurlingham Polo Association) represented England, and won. Thus it was not long before Great Britain found her niche in international polo once more.

Of the country's 24 clubs (including about 750 players) at the end of the '80s – four have been staging high-goal tournaments. Those are the Royal Berkshire, Cirencester Park, Cowdray Park and the Guards. Britain is now one of the strongest and most popular centres of international polo, regularly attracting through each season, half-a-dozen Americans, eight or nine Australians and New Zealanders and a good showing from South American players and Continental Europe. Another addition to British prestige is possession of the world's highest handicap woman player, Claire Tomlinson.

INTERNATIONAL PRECEDENCE

In terms of world priority, after Argentina comes Mexico which, though a country of relatively few players, can field a team of at least 36 goals. The United States might raise a 35-goal and England one of 31, about the same as New Zealand. Australia, Brazil and Chile would be next each with national team capacities of about 24–26. Then Spain, about 23, France, Pakistan and South Africa are probably approximately level at 20–21, then India at 17–18 and Germany and Zimbabwe at 13–14.

HURLINGHAM POLO ASSOCIATION

AFFILIATED CLUBS AND ASSOCIATIONS

GREAT BRITAIN AND EIRE

All Ireland Polo Club
  Phoenix Park, Dublin

Anglesey Polo Club
  Henblas, Bodorgan; also Anglesey
  Show Ground, Mona

Cambridge University Polo Club
  Rutland Club, Oakham,
  Leicestershire

Cheshire Polo Club
  Oulton Grounds, Little Budworth

Cirencester Park Polo Club
  Cirencester Park, Gloucestershire

Colchester Garrison Polo Club
  Ypres Road, Colchester Garrison,
  Essex

Cowdray Park Polo Club
  Cowdray Park, Midhurst, Sussex

Cyprus Polo Association
  British Forces Cyprus,
  c/o Episkopi Polo Club

Dundee and Perth Polo Club
  Scone Palace Polo Ground

Edinburgh Polo Club
  Dalmahoy Park, Midlothian

Epsom Polo Club
  Horton Country Park, Epsom

Guards Polo Club
  Smith's Lawn, Windsor Great
  Park

Ham Polo Club
  Ham House, Petersham, Surrey;
  also Richmond Park

Kirtlington Park Polo Club
  Kirtlington Park, Oxfordshire

Millfield School Polo Club
  Millfield School, Street, Somerset

Oxford University Polo Club
  Kirtlington Park, Oxfordshire

Rhine Army Polo Association
  Bad Lippspringe, West Germany

Rhinefield (New Forest) Polo
Club
  New Park Farm, Brockenhurst,
  Hants

Royal County of Berkshire
Polo Club
  North Street, Winkfield, Windsor

Royal Naval Equestrian
Association
  c/o Taunton Vale Polo Club

Rutland Polo Club
  Rutland Show Ground

Silver Leys Polo Club
  Carver Barracks, Saffron Walden,
  Essex

Taunton Vale Polo Club
  Orchard Portman, near Taunton

Tidworth Polo Club
  Tidworth, Hants

Toulston Polo Club
  Tadcaster, Yorkshire

Whitfield Court Polo Club
  Waterford, Ireland

AUSTRALIAN POLO COUNCIL

New South Wales
  Affiliated Clubs: Goulburn,
  Tamarang, Toompang, County
  Gunnedah, Wirragulla, Quirindi,
  Muswelbrook, Forbes, Tally-Ho,
  Narromine, Wellington, Scone,
  Moree, Willow Tree, Vychan,
  Canberra, Tamworth, Warrun
  Bungle, Windsor, Rylstore

Queensland
  Affiliated Clubs: Downs,
  Goondiwindi, Bulloo, Cannamulla

South Australia
  Affiliated Clubs: Adelaide, Mount
  Crawford,
  Strathalbyn, Broken Hill

Victoria
  Affiliated Clubs: Hexham, Yarra
  Glen/Lilydale, Melbourne,
  Melbourne Hunt (Cranbourne)

Western Australia
  Teams: Perth, Kojonup,
  Serpentine, Walkaway, Capel,
  Condingup

BARBADOS POLO CLUB: Holders, St James, Barbados

ROYAL BRUNEI POLO ASSOCIATION: *Affiliated Clubs:* Jerudong Park, Berakas

GHANA POLO ASSOCIATION: Mile Six, Dodowa Road, Accra

HONG KONG POLO ASSOCIATION: Transferred to Taunton Vale Polo Club

INDIAN POLO ASSOCIATION

Calcutta Polo Club
  Calcutta

Delhi Polo Club
  New Delhi

Rajasthan Polo Club
  Rajasthan

Indian Polo Association
  New Delhi

Remount and Veterinary Corps
Polo Club
  Meerut-Cantt

Amateur Rider Club
  Bombay

Dehra Dun Polo Club
  Dehra Dun

Poona Polo Club
  Poona

Madras Polo and Riders' Club
  Madras

ALL JAMAICA POLO ASSOCIATION: *Affiliated Clubs:* Kingston, St
Ann, Chukka Cove

ROYAL JORDAN POLO CLUB: Amman, Jordan

KENYA POLO ASSOCIATION: *Affiliated Clubs:* Manyatta (Gilgil),
Nairobi, Nanyuki, North Kenya

MALAYAN POLO ASSOCIATION (1978): *Affiliated Clubs:* Armed
  Forces Polo & Riding Club, Iskander, Penang, Royal Pahang, Royal
  Johore, Selangor

MALTA POLO CLUB: Marsa Sports Ground

NEW ZEALAND POLO ASSOCIATION

Northern
Affiliated Clubs: Auckland,
Cambridge, Glen Murray,
Kihikihi, Lanherne, Morrinsville,
Tangiteroria, Taupiri, Waimai

Central Districts
Affiliated Clubs: Hawkes Bay,
Poverty Bay, Rangitikei, Wanstead

South Island
Affiliated Clubs: Amuri, Ashburton,
Ashley, Blenheim, Geraldine

NIGERIAN POLO ASSOCIATION: *Affiliated Clubs:* Lagos, Ibadan,
  Kano, Katsina, Maidiguri, Jos, Port Harcourt, Sokoto, Kaduna, Accra,
  Zaria

ROYAL OMAN POLO CLUB: Oman

PAKISTAN POLO ASSOCIATION

Affiliated Clubs: Abbottabad, Chitral, Gilgit, Karachi, Kharian, Lahore,
Multan, Nowshera, Peshawar, Rawalpindi, Baluchistan, Pakistan
Railway, Punjab Police, Mona, ASC Club

SINGAPORE POLO CLUB: Thomson Road, Singapore 1129

SOUTH AFRICAN POLO ASSOCIATION

Transvaal
Affiliated Clubs: 3 clubs

East Griqualand
Affiliated Clubs: 4 clubs

Natal
Affiliated Clubs: 14 clubs

Orange Free State and Cape
Affiliated Clubs: 10 clubs

ZAMBIA POLO ASSOCIATION: *Affiliated Clubs:* Lusaka, Mazabuka

POLO ASSOCIATION OF ZIMBABWE: *Affiliated Clubs:* Banket,
  Harare, Thornpark, Umboe, Mvurwi

UNITED STATES POLO ASSOCIATION

AFFILIATED CLUBS AND ASSOCIATIONS

UNITED STATES AND CANADA

Aiken Polo Club
  Aiken, South Carolina

Amwell Valley Country Club
  Neshanic Station, New Jersey

Aspen Polo Club
  Aspen, Colorado

Atlanta Polo Club
  Atlanta, Georgia

Austin Polo Club
  Austin, Texas

Avalon Polo Club
  Tulsa, Oklahoma

Baton Rouge Polo Assn.
  Baton Rouge, Louisiana

Bellingham Polo Club
  Bellingham, Washington

Big Horn Polo Club
  Big Horn, Wyoming

Blackberry Polo Club
  Batavia, Illinois

Blue Water Creek
  Polo Club
  Muscle Shoals, Alabama

Brandywine Polo Assn.
  Toughkenamon, Pennsylvania

Broad Acres Polo Club
  Norman, Oklahoma

Brookside Polo Club
  Vernon, New York

Bull Run Polo Club
  Cliffton, Virginia

Burnt Mills Polo Club
  Bedminster, New Jersey

Calgary Polo Club
  Calgary, Alberta

Camden Polo Club
  Camden, South Carolina

Cape Cod Polo Club
  East Falmouth, Massachusetts

Central Florida Polo Club
  Orlando, Florida

Central Valley Polo Club
  Turlock, California

Charleston Polo Club
  Charleston, South Carolina

Charlotte Polo Club
  Charlotte, North Carolina

Charlottesville Polo Club
  Charlottesville, Virginia

Chattanooga Polo Assn.
  Chattanooga, Tennessee

Cheyenne Polo Club
  Cheyenne, Wyoming

Chukker Downs Polo Club
  Rougemont, North Carolina

Cincinnati Polo Club
  Cincinnati, Ohio

Cleveland Polo Club
  Gates Mills, Ohio

Columbia Polo Club
  Columbia, South Carolina

Columbus Polo Club
  Columbus, Georgia

Columbus Polo Club of Ohio
  Columbus, Ohio

Covington Polo Club
  Covington, Louisiana

Darlington Polo Club
  Darlington, Pennsylvania

Dayton Polo Club
  Dayton, Ohio

Denver Polo Club
  Littleton, Colorado

Derry Heir Farm Polo Club
  Moreland Hills, Ohio

Des Moines Polo Club
  Des Moines, Iowa

Detroit Polo Club
  Milford, Michigan

Down East Polo Club
  South Harpswell, Maine

Duluth Polo Club
  Duluth, Minnesota

Eldorado Polo Club
  Indio, California

Empire Polo Club
  Indio, California

Eugene Polo Club
  Coburg, Oregon

Fairfield Polo Association
  Wichita, Kansas

Fair Hills Polo &
  Hunt Club
  Topanga, California

Fairlane Farms at Wellington
  West Palm Beach, Florida

Far Hills Polo Club
  Lebanon, New Jersey

Farmington Hunt Club
  Charlottesville, Virginia

Folsom Polo Club
  New Orleans, Louisiana

Fort Stotsenburg Polo Club
  Clark Air Force Base, Philippines

Fort Worth Polo Club
  Forth Worth, Texas

Foxhall Polo Club
  Carrollton, Georgia

Fox Lea Farm Polo Club
  Rehoboth, Massachusetts

Garrod Polo Farms
  Saratoga, California

Glendale Polo Club
  Glen Ellyn, Illinois

Gold Coast Arena Polo Club
  Locust Valley, New York

Golden Isles Polo Club
  St. Simons Isle, Georgia

Gone Away Farm Polo Club
Poolesville, Maryland

Grande Prairie Polo Club
Grande Prairie, AB., Canada

Greater Grand Rapids Polo Club
Grand Rapids, Michigan

Green Acres Polo Club
Dover, New Hampshire

Greenbriar Polo Club
Sacramento, California

Greene Valley Polo Club
Naperville, Illinos

Greenwich Polo Club
Greenwich, Connecticut

Gulfport Polo Club
Gulfport, Mississippi

Gulfstream Polo Club
Lake Worth, Florida

Hardschuffle Polo Club
Louisville, Kentucky

Harrah's Polo Club
Smithville, New Jersey

Hart Ranch Polo Club
Rapid City, South Dakota

Hawaii Polo Club at
Mokuleia
Honolulu, Hawaii

Healy Farms Polo Club
Northbrook, Illinois

Hilton Head Polo Club
Bluffton, South Carolina

Horseworld Polo Club
Scottsdale, Arizona

Houston Polo Association
Houston, Texas

Iowa City Polo Club
Iowa City, Iowa

Jackson Hole Polo Club
Jackson, Wyoming

Jackson Polo Club
Jackson, Mississippi

Joy Farm Polo Club
Milwaukee, Wisconsin

K and T Ranch Polo Club
Grass Valley, California

Kansas City Polo Club
Kansas City, Missouri

Kauai Polo Club
Lihue, Kauai, Hawaii

Kentree Polo Club
Grand Rapids, Michigan

Kentucky Polo Assn. Lexington
Chapter
Lexington, Kentucky

Kentucky Polo Assn. Louisville
Chapter
Louisville, Kentucky

Krazy Horse Polo Club
Scottsdale, Arizona

LaJolla Polo Club
LaJolla, California

La Mariposa Polo Club
Tucson, Arizona

Lancaster Polo Club
Rothsville, Pennsylvania

Las Anitas Polo Club
Chihuahua, Mexico

Lone Star Polo Club
Katy, Texas

Longwood Polo Club
Carmel, Indiana

Los Angeles Polo Club
Los Angeles, California

Los Potros Polo Club
Pilot Point, Texas

Mad River Polo Club
Korbel, California

Mahoning Valley Polo Club
Canfield, Ohio

Malibu Polo Club
Malibu, California

Mallet Hill Polo Club
Cochranville, Pennsylvania

Maryland Polo Club
Monkton, Maryland

Maui Polo Club, Inc.
Kahului, Hawaii

Mauna Kea Polo Club
Kamuela, Hawaii

Meadowbrook Polo
Club, Inc.
Jericho, L.I., New York

Memphis Polo Association
Memphis, Tennessee

Menlo Polo Club
Menlo Park, California

Middleburg Polo Club
Middleburg, Virginia

Midfield Polo Club
Camden, South Carolina

Midland Polo Club
Midland, Texas

Midway Polo Club
Livermore, California

Midwest Polo Center
Naperville, Illinois

Millbrook Polo Club
Millbrook, New York

Milwaukee Polo Club, Inc.
Milwaukee, Wisconsin

Mobile Point Clear Polo Club
Mobile, Alabama

Modesto Polo Club
Modesto, California

Monterrey Polo Club
Monterrey, N.L., Mexico

Montreal Polo Club
Hudson, Quebec

Moorpark Polo Club
Moorpark, California

Myopia Hunt Club
So. Hamilton, Massachusetts

Napa Polo Club
San Francisco, California

Naperville Polo Club
Naperville, Illinois

Naperville Women's Polo Club
Naperville, Illinois

Nashville Polo Assn., Inc.
Nashville, Tennessee

National Capital Park Polo Club
Washington, D.C.

Newport Polo Club
Newport, Rhode Island

Northshore Polo Club
LaComb, Louisiana

Oak Brook Polo Club
Oak Brook, Illinois

Oak Grove Polo Club
Decatur, Texas

Oak Hill Farms
Plano, Texas

Ocala Polo Club
Ocala, Florida

Olympia Polo Club
Oconomowoc, Wisconsin

Orlando Polo Club
Orlando, Florida

Owl Creek Polo Club
Scotia, New York

Ox Ridge Hunt Club
Darien, Connecticut

Palm Beach Polo and Country Club
West Palm Beach, Florida

Paradise Valley
Polo Club
Cave Creek, Arizona

Paso Del Norte Polo Assn.
El Paso, Texas

Pebble Beach Polo Club
Pebble Beach, California

Peoria Polo Club
Chillicothe, Illinois

Pierre Polo Club
Pierre, South Dakota

Pima County Polo Club
Tucson, Arizona

Pinehurst Polo Club
Southern Pine, North Carolina

Plum Creek Polo Club
Sedalia, Colorado

Polo Club of Chicago, Inc.
Chicago, Illinois

Polo Club of Jacksonville
Jacksonville, Florida

Polo Hill Polo Club
Annandale, New Jersey

Potomac Polo Club
Rockville, Maryland

Princeton Polo Club
Princeton, New Jersey

Quechee Polo Club
Quechee, Vermont

Queen City Polo Club
Cincinnati, Ohio

Ramapo Hunt & Polo Club
Mahwah, New Jersey

Rancho Deluxe
Arroyo Grande, California

Rancho Naranjo Polo Club
Santa Teresa, New Mexico

Rancho Santa Fe Polo Club
LaJolla, California

Rappahannock Polo Club
Castleton, Virginia

Red Rock Rangers Polo Club
Monument, Colorado

Retama Polo Center
San Antonio, Texas

Rio Grande Polo Club
Kingsville, Texas

Rockford Polo Club
Rockford, Illinois

Rose Hill Plantation
Polo Club
Bluffton, South Carolina

Royal Palm Polo Club
Boca Raton, Florida

St. Louis Country Club
Clayton, Missouri

Sacramento Valley Polo Club
Sacramento, California

Sagebrush Polo Club
Litchfield, California

Salem Valley Polo Club
Salem, Connecticut

San Antonio Polo Club
San Antonio, Texas

San Mateo-Burlingame Polo Club
San Mateo, California

San Patricio Polo Club
San Patricio, New Mexico

San Saba Polo Club
San Saba, Texas

Santa Barbara Polo Club
Santa Barbara, California

Santa Fe Polo Grounds
Santa Fe, New Mexico

Santa Rosa Polo Club
Santa Rosa, California

Santa Ynez Valley Polo Club
Buellton, California

Saratoga Polo Assn., Ltd.
Greenfield, New York

Seattle Polo Club
Seattle, Washington

Sewickley Polo Club
Sewickley, Pennsylvania

Shallowbrook Polo Club
Somers, Connecticut

Show Park Polo Club
Rancho Santa Fe, California

Skaneateles Polo Club
Skaneateles, New York

Southeastern Polo Club
Alpharetta, Georgia

Spokane Polo Club
Spokane, Washington

Spring Hills Polo and Saddle Club
Dallas, Texas

Springfield Polo Club
Dugald, Manitoba

Sugarbush Polo Club
Waitsfield, Vermont

Sun Valley Polo Club
Sun Valley, Idaho

Sunnyland Polo Club
Loxahatchee, Florida

Tampa Bay Polo Club
Temple Terrace, Florida

Tanglewood Polo Club
Hillsborough, North Carolina

Texas A&M Polo Club
Wellborn, Texas

Tongg Ranch Polo Club
Honolulu, Hawaii

Toronto Polo Club
Toronto, Canada

Tri Valley Polo Club
Encino, California

Tulsa Polo & Hunt Club
Tulsa, Oklahoma

Twin City Polo Club
Maple Plain, Minnesota

Unadilla Polo Club
Unadilla, New York

Ventura Polo Club
Ventura, California

Village Farms Polo Club
Gilbertsville, New York

Virginia Beach Polo Club
Virginia Beach, Virginia

Waimanalo Polo Club
Waimanalo, Hawaii

West Hills Polo Club
Huntington, New York 11743

West River Polo Club
So. Londonderry, Vermont

West Shore Polo Club
Mechanicsburg, Pennsylvania

White Ash Polo Club
Plainfield, Illinois

Will Rogers Polo Club
Los Angeles, California

Willow Bend Polo & Hunt Club
Plano, Texas

Windsford Polo Club
Dickerson, Maryland

Winston Polo Club
Anaheim, California

Yale Polo Association
Essex, Connecticut

SCHOOLS AND COLLEGES

Colorado State University Polo
Club
Fort Collins, Colorado

Cornell Polo Club
Ithaca, New York

Culver Military Academy
Culver, Indiana

Florida Atlantic University
Boca Raton, Florida

Garrison Forest School
Garrison, Maryland

Harvard University Polo Club
Cambridge, Massachusetts

Lawrenceville Polo Club
Lawrenceville, New Jersey

Middlebury College
Middlebury, Vermont

Pace University Polo Club
Pleasantville, New York

Skidmore College
Saratoga Springs, New York

SMU Polo Club
Dallas, Texas

Stanford University
Stanford, California

Texas A&M Polo Club
College Station, Texas

Texas Tech
Lubbock, Texas

Tulane University
New Orleans, Louisiana

University of Arizona
Tucson, Arizona

University of California Davis Polo
Club
Davis, California

University of Connecticut
Storrs, Connecticut

University of Kentucky
Lexington, Kentucky

University of Southern California
Los Angeles, California

University of Texas
Austin, Texas

University of Virginia
Charlottesville, Virginia

Valley Forge Military Academy
Wayne, Pennsylvania

Yale Univ. Polo Association
New Haven, Connecticut

OTHER AFFILIATE MEMBERS

Chukka Cove Polo Club
  Ocho Rios
  Jamaica, W.I.

Ingenio Polo Club
  Santurce, Puerto Rico

Romans Polo Club
  La Romana,
  Dominica Republic

Manila Polo Club
  Manila, P.I.

RULES OF POLO

After the International Rules had been drafted in 1938 for the International Rules Committee, in association with the Chairmen of the principal Polo Associations, the United States Polo Association found themselves unable to ratify them. This led to some differences in the wording and numbering of Rules and Penalties, which have persisted since the Hurlingham Polo Association took over the International Rules in 1875.

A summary of the Penalties used by both associations is given below. The main differences will be found in Penalties 7, 8 and 9. The USPA Penalty 1 automatically includes Penalty 3, and their Penalty 3 can be the same as their Penalty 2 if the Captain of the fouled side elects to take the hit from where the foul occurred.

The HPA Penalty 7 collects the cases of infringements of the Rules in carrying out penalties, whereas the USPA leaves particulars under the various penalties. The HPA have no Penalty to forfeit the match corresponding to USPA Penalty 9.

In 1938 every Penalty in the International Rules was given a short name as well as a number (e.g. Penalty 3—40 Yard Hit) which was not adopted by the USPA. The most important rule in Polo, Field Rule 16, dealing with 'crossing' was clarified in the HPA rules but in effect has the same intention as USPA Field Rule 16.

Really there is no serious discrepancy between the two sets of Rules and Penalties but Players, and even more so Umpires, on crossing the Atlantic, would be well advised to glance at the summary below and then read the full Rules under which they will play or umpire.

HURLINGHAM POLO ASSOCIATION PENALTIES

1 **Penalty Goal** If a player commits a dangerous or deliberate foul to save a goal, Side fouled receive one goal. Ends not changed. Restart by bowling ball in, 10 yards from middle of Foulers' goal towards either side.

2   **30 Yard Hit** Ball either 30 yards opposite goal or where foul occurred (fouled Captain's choice). Foulers behind back line, or at least 30 yards from ball; not to ride out through goal. Side fouled behind ball.

3   **40 Yard Hit** Ball 40 yards opposite goal. Foulers behind back line; not to ride out through goal. Side fouled behind ball.

4   **60 Yard Hit (opposite goal)** Ball 60 yards opposite goal. Foulers to be at least 30 yards from ball; side fouled anywhere.

5(a) **Free Hit (from Spot)** Ball on spot where foul occurred but not within 4 yards of boards or side lines. Foulers to be at least 30 yards from ball; side fouled anywhere.

5(b) **Free Hit (from Centre)** Ball in centre of ground. Foulers to be at least 30 yards from ball; side fouled anywhere.

6   **60 Yard Hit (from where ball crosed)** Ball on 60 yard line opposite where it crossed back line, but not within 4 yards of boards or side lines. Foulers to be at least 30 yards from ball; side fouled anywhere.

7(a) **Another Hit** If Foulers infringe Penalties 2 to 6 carry out penalty again unless goal awarded. If both sides infringe Penalties 2 or 3 carry out penalty again irrespective of result of previous Free Hit.

7(b) **Hit in by Defenders** If side fouled infringe Penalties 2 or 3 Defenders hit in from middle of own goal. Attackers to be at least 30 yards from back line; Defenders anywhere.

7(c) **Hit in from 30 Yard Line** If attackers cross 30 yard line before a 'Hit in' ball is moved straight forward to 30 yard line and Attackers hit in from there. Attackers to be at least 30 yards from ball; Defenders anywhere.

7(d) **Unnecessary Delay** If unnecessary delay by side fouled to take hit, in Penalties 2 to 5, restart game by bowling ball in from previous spot towards side of ground.

8   **Player to Retire** Player nearest above handicap of disabled player designated by fouled Captain to retire. Foulers must continue with three players or forfeit match.

9(a) **Pony Disqualified** A pony blind of an eye, showing vice or not under proper control is disqualified and ordered off (HPA Field Rule 3).

9(b) **Pony Ordered Off** If a pony's equipment infringes HPA Field Rule 4 it is ordered off until offence has been removed.

9 (c) Player Ordered Off If a player infringes HPA Field Rule 5 he is ordered off until he has removed sharp spurs or buckles or studs.

> **NOTE** In penalties 9(a), (b) and (c) play must be restarted immediately in accordance with Field Rule 25 (*i.e.* ball bowled in towards nearest side from where it was when whistle was blown).

10   Player Excluded Player ordered off for deliberate dangerous foul or prejudicial conduct. His side must continue with three or forfeit match.

UNITED STATES POLO ASSOCIATION PENALTIES

1 (a) If player commits dangerous or deliberate foul to save a goal, Side fouled awarded a goal, and given Penalty 3.

(b) If goal prevented by Foulers infringing rules goal is scored.

(c) If Foulers infringe rules but no goal was hit Side fouled repeat free hit.

(d) If Side fouled infringe rules Foulers hit in from centre of goal line; other side at least 30 yards from ball.

(e) If both Sides infringe rules repeat the penalty.

2 (a) Ball either 30 yards opposite goal or where foul occurred (fouled Captain's choice). Foulers behind back line or at least 30 yards from ball, not to ride through goal. Side fouled behind ball.

(b), (c), (d) and **(e)** same as **Penalty 1**.

3   Identical with Penalty 2 but for '30 yards' read '40 yards'.

4 (a) Free Hit at ball 60 yards opposite goal. Foulers to be at least 30 yards from ball; Side fouled anywhere.

(b) If Foulers infringe rules and no goal is scored Side fouled repeat penalty.

5 (a) Free Hit at ball from point where foul occurred or from Centre of Field (Umpire's decision). Foulers to be at least 30 yards from ball; Side fouled anywhere.

(b) If Foulers' infringe rules and no goal is scored Side fouled repeat penalty.

> **NOTE** There are two paragraphs at the end of Penalties dealing with the Intent for use of the two positions of the Ball in Penalty 5.

6 (a) Free Hit at ball on 60 yard line opposite where it crossed back line. Foulers to be at least 30 yards from ball, Side fouled anywhere.

(b) If Foulers infringe rules and no goal is scored Side fouled repeat penalty.

7 Player nearest above handicap of disabled player designated by fouled Captain to retire. No change in handicap given at start. Foulers must continue with three players or forfeit match.

8 Pony ordered off and disqualified from playing again. If for infringement of USPA Field Rule 3 (e.g. heel caulks on front shoes) pony may play again after removal of offence provided game is not delayed.

9 Match forfeited.

10 Player excluded for deliberate dangerous foul or prejudicial conduct. His Side must continue with three.

BASIC EQUIPMENT
Retailer's Price List and List of Suppliers

For the Player

	£UK	$US
Cap	£70–£85	$60–$90
Faceguard	£20–£30	$15–$30
Breeches	£45–£55	$40–$75
Boots	£180–£300	$180–$500
Spurs	£18–£40	$15–$30
Whip	£9–£25	$25–$50
Gloves	£19–£22	$20–$35
Shirt	£19–£25	$30–$40

For the Pony

	£UK	$US
Bridle with reins + bit	£90–£120	$125–$175
Martingale	£20–£29	$50–$75
'Gracida' [Polo] saddle	£350–£400	$400–$900
Girth	£9–£35	$35–$50
Buffalo leathers	£26–£29	$35–$70
Stirrup irons	£17–£20	$20–$30
Breast girth [plate]	£25–£28	$50–$75
Surcingle	£21–£23	$35–$50
Saddle cloth [pad]	£16–£18	$20–$30
Bandages (set of 4)	£13–£15	$15–$20
or Porter [protective] boots (4)	£27–£30	$45–$75
New Zealand rug	£40–£70	$125–$150
Stable rug [blanket]	£25–£40	$80–$100
Head collar [halter] and lead	£12–£20	$20–$45

United Kingdom Equipment Suppliers

The Polo Shop,
Lodsworth,
Nr Petworth,
West Sussex. Tel: 07985–585

J. Salter & Son,
23 High Street,
Aldershot GU11 1BH. Tel: 0252–25692

W. & H. Gidden Ltd,
15D Clifford Street,
London W1X 1RF. Tel: 01–734 2788

United States Equipment Suppliers

Miller Harness Co., Inc.,
235 Murray Hill Parkway,
E. Rutherford, NJ 07073

Meurisse, Gordon & Co., Inc.,
202 W. North Ave.,
Lombard, IL 60148

Midwest Saddlery Co.,
4415 'B' Dr., S.,
Battle Creek, MI 49017

T.E.C. Polo,
741 W. Jericho Turnpike,
Huntington, NY 11743

Smith Worthington Saddlery Co.,
287 Homestead Ave.,
Hartford, CT 06112.

Texas Polo,
703 McKinney Ave.,
Suite 100,
Dallas, TX 75202.

FURTHER READING
For the Aficionado and the Beginner

Bent, Newell, *American Polo*, Macmillan, 1929. *A comprehensive history up to the late 1920s.*

Board, John, *Polo*, Faber, 1956. *A survey of the game with excellent instructive drawings by the author.*

Brooke, Geoffrey, *The Way of a Man with a Horse*, in the Lonsdale Library series, Seeley Service, 1929. *Includes a chapter on polo ponies, by one of the greatest horsemasters of his time.*

Dawnay, Hugh, *Polo Vision*, J. A. Allen, 1984. *The game's tactics and the acquiring and keeping of ponies as taught by the author at his Whitfield Court school in Co. Waterford.*

Gannon, Jack, *Before the Colours Fade*, J. A. Allen, 1976. *Brief autobiography by the manager and secretary of the Hurlingham Club in the 1930s. He was well known during the post-war years for his articles in* The Field *and* Horse and Hound. *Contains a first-hand account of the polo encounters in the 1936 Berlin Olympics.*

Kimberley, Earl of (ed), *Polo*, (Lonsdale Library Vol XXI) Seeley Service, 1930. *With contributions by Brig.-Gen. G. Beresford, Major-Gen. Geoffrey Brooke, Lt.-Col. Jack Gannon, 'Marco', Brig.-Gen. R. L. Ricketts and P. Vischer.*

Kipling, Rudyard, *The Maltese Cat*, Macmillan, 1898. *The author's classic with a polo pony hero in the 1890s. Included in his collection of stories, entitled* The Day's Work. *Macmillan produced a special edition, with drawings by Lionel Edwards, in 1955.*

Lyon, W. E., *First Aid Hints for the Horse Owner*, Collins, 1933–65. *A sound veterinary guide, which was revised eight times, the ninth edition being published in 1965.*

'Marco', *An Introduction to Polo*, Country Life, 1931. *Lord Mountbatten's classic which went into five subsequent editions.*

Vickers, Lt.-Gen. W. G., *Practical Polo*, J. A. Allen, 1958. *A simple guide, illustrated, demonstratively, with 'stick' men and 'stick ponies'.*

Watson, J. N. P., *The World of Polo: Past and Present*, Sportsman's Press, 1986. *A description of the game and a detailed history of it. Profusely illustrated.*

Publications regularly reporting the game in Britain. *The Times, Daily Telegraph, Country Life, Horse and Hound*

Publications regularly reporting the game in the United States *The Chronicle Of the Horse, Polo, Pro Polo, Polo International, Horse World USA, National Polo Journal*

INDEX